From Sickology
to a

Healthy Logic

Dominiquae Bierman, PhD

Author of *The Identity Theft*

Published by Zion's Gospel Press

52 Tuscan Way, Ste 202-412
St. Augustine, FL, 32092
shalom@zionsgospel.com

Paperback ISBN: 978-1-953502-35-3
E-Book ISBN: 978-1-953502-36-0

On occasion words such as Jesus, Christ, Lord and God have been changed by the author, back to their original Hebrew renderings, Yeshua, Messiah, Yahveh, and Elohim.

Bold or italicized emphasis or underlining within quotations is the author's own.

Printed in the United States of America

First Printing April 2009, Second Printing April 2011, June 2021

Thanksgiving

I want to thank, first and foremost, my Father in Heaven and Yeshua my Jewish Messiah who have carried me through in victory, in spite of much suffering and many setbacks. He also surrounded me with prayer, the prayer of many people throughout the world. I do not know all of your names, but you know who you are, thank you!

I also thank my amazing team at the Eilat Prayer Tower during the years of 2009-2015, especially Phyllis Lines, Gale and Yitschak Reed, Terhi Mäkinen, Esther Kohen, Betty Adame and many more that came and went and helped us when Yuval was recovering! Your efforts are bearing *much* fruit! HaleluYah! To Abigail (Maria Trinidad) who took care of my daughter Adi during one of the most difficult bouts of depression.

A special thanks to a unique, one of a kind lady who helped me through the darkest time of my life after Yuval's worst suicide attempt, Karen Wilson. She was my secretary, housekeeper and watchman around Yuval's hospital bed. She did so many difficult things that no one else would have done. Karen, I love you and I will never forget you. My prayers for your eternal wellbeing are with you!

I thank Malka (Stephanie East) and Debra Barnes for the faithful work of proofreading and Esther Kohen for the layout and graphics. These wonderful ladies worked for many hours selflessly on this book. Bless you!

One very important person deserves my thanks for eternity. My dear Doris, you have been one of the most important gifts that Elohim has granted us. Your unparalleled generosity, dedication, friendship and practical wisdom have helped our family through times of terrible ordeals. I have no words to describe my gratitude. You have my constant prayers for your wellbeing, and I pray God will grant you to reap the love and support that you sowed into my children, my husband and me. Be blessed, you and your family forever!

Last, but certainly not least, I want to thank my very faithful husband Rabbi Baruch Bierman who has accompanied me through thick and thin and has been a rock of support and faith to me and to my children! You are an unparalleled husband! Thank you honey!

Dedication

I DEDICATE THIS BOOK to my faithful husband, Rabbi Baruch Bierman. He has stood with me through thick and thin as I catered to my children and others with mental problems and challenges. He walked with me, countless times, as we visited my loved ones in mental hospitals. He has never complained about the many difficulties and superhuman efforts that were required, but instead, always exhibited faith and an optimistic disposition.

He has earned the title of Pops from my son Yuval and Baruchi (my Baruch or my Blessing) from my daughter Adi. Although he is not their biological father, he has been their consistent father, showing unconditional love and support since they were two (Yuval) and five (Adi) years old. Their orphan hood was overturned by his faithfulness!

Honey, you deserve a crown of glory. I love you!

Disclaimer

I am not a psychologist or a psychiatrist. I rather bring the biblical perspective of my understanding on psychological issues. Even though sometimes it may seem that I expose psychiatry and psychology in an unfavorable light, please rest assured that I am convinced that many psychiatrists and psychologists are very sacrificial people and they exercise their profession in order to help people and not necessarily because of the money factor.

I also believe that many of them have helped people who otherwise would have had nowhere else to turn. In fact, I believe that in some cases, psychiatric *first aid* can be very vital, just like physical first aid, in the case of an accident or an emergency.

The problem arises when it goes further to provide the cure through meds and psychoanalysis without God, His Words or His instructions. I have seen most of the psychiatrists and psychologists who I have encountered put their trust in meds or psychoanalysis solely, thus replacing The Creator for human created medicine, devices and chemicals. This has shaped an entire generation that turns to meds and psychologists instead of to Elohim-God-The Creator, His Word, His Spirit and His ways.

There are many branches of Psychology today. Some of the branches are closer to the Word of God than others, so it seems unfair to put them all 'in the same basket' so to speak. However, I am dealing with the *spirit* and *root* of Psychology and Psychiatry in general, so I apologize in advance if you are a Godly Psychologist who has put The Word of God above Freudian and other theories that you have spent years studying. I commend you for that! My hope is that, in the future, many psychologists will do that and work with Holy Spirit empowered ministers of the Gospel to bring true healing to their patients.

Respectfully,
–Archbishop Dr. Dominiquae Bierman

CONTENTS

Chapter 1: My Interaction with Suicide 1

My Story 2

My Daughter Adi 4

Adi Tells Her Story: 6

My Son Yuval 7

Yuval Tells His Story 12

Chapter 2: Suicide In the Bible 15

Samson – Suicide or an Act of Bravery? 15

King Saul – Suicide as an Act of Honor 19

Ahithophel – Suicide as a Response to Offended Pride . . 21

Elijah – The Great Prophet Who Wanted to Die 24

Judas – Suicide as the Ultimate Act of Betrayal 27

Chapter 3: Exposing Existentialism 37

The Religion of Unbelief & Restoring a Healthy Logic . . 37

Existentialism 40

Jewish Existentialism Is Hitler's "Child" 42

The Mistaken Starting Point 44

Psychology Comes to the "Rescue"? 45

Repentance Leads to Freedom 46

Chapter 4: The Futility of Life? 49

The Fruit of Psychology & Existentialism 52

A Money Making Machine 54

Existentialism Is a Type of Satanic Worship 56

The Antidote To The Deadly Sick Logic 57

Chapter 5: The Power of the Word 61

True Stability 62

What You Believe Determines Your Mental Health! 63

Faith In Money 64

Faith In Myself 65

Faith In Religion 66

Faith In the Universe 68

The Only Proven Stable Object of Faith In the World . . . 69

Chapter 6: The Great Transformation 73

The Plumb-Line of Trust! 74

Petitions: Faith In His Word 76

Supplication: Faith In His Nature 78

Thanksgiving: Faith In His Ability to Act 79

Review 80

Chapter 7: What Are You Leaning On? 81

Supermen & Women Can Break! 82

Mind of Messiah 86

Chapter 8: The Baptism In the Holy Spirit 89

The Baptism In the Holy Spirit 89

A Shower From Heaven! 91

Praying In Tongues 94

Important Disclaimer! 95

Chapter 9: Spiritual Warfare................... 97
Weapons of Warfare 100

Chapter 10: On Purpose – Davka!............. 103
Davka – Do Not Surrender to the Curse! 104
Rejoice on Purpose!................... 105
Walking In Love Davka Makes You Whole............ 108
Speak Faith................... 113

Chapter 11: Faith Is Work!................... 115
It's Easier to Take a Pill, But Is it the Life You Want? 116
Do the Work of Faith & Inherit a Life of Wholeness! ... 116
An Important Disclaimer................... 117
The Faith of Abraham Leaves the Familiar Behind! 117
Removing the Mystery of Schizophrenia 119
Perseverance Is the Key................... 123
Faith Speaks, Acts, & Shows on Purpose: Davka! 123
A Declaration of Commitment 124
Do You Believe?................... 125

Chapter 12: Caregivers: Buckle Yourself First 127
Stubbornness & Rebellion................... 128
Buckle Yourself First 131
Periodical Maintenance 133
Beware of Kryptonite – Rotate Caregivers!........... 134
The Priestly Blessing................... 136
Contact Us................... 136

Appendix A: What Is Replacement Theology? 137

Appendix B: The Names of God 139

Appendix C: Other Books. 141

xiv

Introduction

Shalom! Wellbeing, wholeness, peace, and blessing to you! This book is the product of 18 years of walking through psychiatric hospitals catering to my loved ones. I have seen, prayed and visited with countless mentally sick patients. I have talked with many psychiatrists and psychologists. I have had to fight for the mental wellbeing psychiatrists and psychologists. I have had to fight for the mental wellbeing of my own loved ones, including my mother, my brother, my children and some of my spiritual children and disciples.

However, my personal experiences would have not been enough to write this book. The Word of God is the Highest Authority as the textbook on the Human Mind. After all, it was Elohim, The Creator of Heaven and Earth, who created our minds! Of course, He did not leave us without an instruction manual!

Therefore, above all psychology, and any other "ology", is The Word of God. In it you will find all the answers to the woes and illnesses of Mankind. The Great News is that this Eternal Book contains *the cure*, and therefore, my purpose is that you will find the infallible and eternal cure for all distressed minds.

In His amazing love,
Archbishop Dr. Dominiquae Bierman

CHAPTER ONE

My Interaction with Suicide

I have decided to start this book with the heaviest and most difficult of subjects, namely the extremely painful act of suicide. In chapter two we will study some biblical cases of suicide, however, in this chapter I will talk about reality today. So let us first review some statistics.

Youth Suicide Statistics (in the USA):

- Suicide is the second leading cause of death for ages 10-24.[*] Suicide is the second leading cause of death for college-age youth.[**]
- More teenagers and young adults die from suicide than from cancer, heart disease, AIDS, birth defects, stroke, pneumonia, influenza, and chronic lung disease, combined.[***]

---

[*] cdc.gov/injury/wisqars/, Accessed 27 Sept. 2016

[**] Ibid

[***] jasonfoundation.com/prp/facts/youth-suicide-statistics/, Accessed 27 Sept. 2016

- Each day in our nation there are over five thousand, four hundred attempts made by young people grades 7-12.[*]
- Four out of Five teens who attempt suicide have given clear warning signs.[**]

General Statistics [***]

- Suicide was the tenth leading cause of death for all ages in 2013.
- There were forty-one thousand, one hundred and forty nine suicides in 2013 in the United States—a rate of 12.6 per 100,000 is equal to one hundred and thirteen suicides each day or one every 13 minutes.
- Based on data about suicides in 16 National Violent Death Reporting System states in 2010, 33.4% of suicide decedents tested positive for alcohol, 23.8% for antidepressants, and 20.0% for opiates, including heroin and prescription pain killers.
- Suicide results in an estimated $fifty one billion in combined medical and work loss costs. Now that we know the discouraging statistics, it is time to research the *root cause* of the plague called *suicide*, but first *my story…*

---

[*] Ibid

[**] Ibid

[***] cdc.gov/violenceprevention/pdf/suicide-datasheet-a.PDF, Accessed 27 Sept. 2016

My Story

The father of my two beautiful children committed suicide after years of suffering from manic-depression. We divorced prior to his death and through the very painful process preceding the divorce, Yeshua (Jesus), the Jewish Messiah, revealed Himself to me and rescued me from sin, hopelessness and death.

Following my salvation experience, I sought to reconcile with my husband even if that meant paying a high personal price. He completely refused on the grounds that I had become a radical believer and follower of Yeshua. My children were in his custody since he was living in the very comfortable house of his parents in one of the richest suburbs of Israel, while I had nothing and was all alone, except for my God and my Faith that is!

A short time after my divorce and my encounter with Yeshua, I met my husband (Rabbi Baruch) with whom I am married till this day. With him I have served YHVH (the Lord) by traveling to preach the Gospel, The Wonderful News that Yeshua, the Jewish Messiah is the Savior of Mankind, to more than 50 nations. Rabbi Baruch adopted my two children into his heart and has cared for them, and for me, throughout all the very difficult periods of our lives. (For the details of my personal story, see my testimony book titled *YES!*)

At a certain point while Baruch and I were in bible school in the USA, Ardon, the father of my children, had a talk with me on the phone from Israel. His question was: Are you still with the Messianic Jews? (Jews who believe in Yeshua-Jesus The Messiah). I answered a resolute *yes* and he retorted, *"Me too, but not the way you think!"*

Then he proceeded to explain how when he exercised his profession of Israeli Tour Guide, he had many Israel loving Christians and Messianic Jews who were his clients and treated him very well giving him lots of substantial tips, but he added that they entreated him again and again to *repent* and turn to Yeshua for salvation. Then he proceeded to tell me the following words, which happen to be the last words that I heard from him before he took his life: *"I will never repent!"*

A terrible chill pierced my body and soul when he categorically said these words. I cried out to him the last words he was to ever hear from me: *"Please, please do not be prideful against Elohim!"*

Ardon killed himself a couple of days after telling me that he will *never repent*. He left behind a seven year old son and a ten year old daughter who were going to suffer the consequences of his pride against the Creator of man. No one lives in a spiritual vacuum. If we reject Elohim's salvation we are automatically accepting Satan's ways and they lead to death and hell.

Pride goes before destruction, and a haughty spirit before a fall.

Proverbs 16:18 NKJV

As you keep reading this book, we will discover the *root cause* for suicide and the *root cause* for all mental sickness.

My Daughter Adi

My daughter was very close to her father and was methodically alienated from me and my faith by parts of her paternal family.

She refused to talk to me or to be with me for four very long years. Eventually, after her father's suicide, she fell into a terrible depression and was hospitalized by her paternal grandparents (with whom she resided) in fear that she may attempt suicide. She was admitted to and released from many mental hospital wards for several years. She was not getting any better. At times she was like a vegetable, not responding to her surroundings, exhibiting a staunch refusal to shower or to eat. My husband and I spent numerous days in these hospitals tending to her and proclaiming God's Word over her life in prayer.

At a certain point the doctor called me aside to tell me the following, "Mrs. Bierman, your daughter is not responding to any medication. I am afraid that she will never have her intellectual abilities like in the past."

I looked at the doctor and said, "Dr. Efrat, you do what you know to do, and I will do what I know to do, and my God will take her out of this terrible predicament!" One and a half years later this same psychiatrist told me the following, *"Your Elohim did it!"*

Even though Adi had not put her trust in Yeshua, she was beginning to implement some faith instructions that I had drilled into her when she was like a "vegetable" and unresponsive. I taught her to forgive, to honor me as her mother and to be thankful to God for every little thing. Adi fully reconciled with me and began to listen to my faith instructions - this was one of the most determining factors in her remarkable recovery.

One day we took her to Office Depot while she was still in very bad shape mentally. She had been the best student in her class prior to these hospitalizations as she loved to study, but now she had completely lost hope of ever amounting to anything intellectually or academically. She was 16 years old and had no hope of ever graduating from high school!

As she sat despondently on the stairs of Office Depot, I filled a cart with everything she would ever need in the way of school supplies. I bought enough to take her all the way through *university*!

She looked at me despondently and said, "Ima (Mom) why are you wasting your money? You know what the doctors said. I will not be able to study or amount to anything." I answered her, "Adi, you will study all the way through *university* because of God's Covenant with me! He promised me that He will deliver you! So you'd better start believing!"

As I am writing these words, my daughter is finishing her master's degree in Special Education and has used every one of the school supplies that I bought her when she was sixteen! When she received her BA in Education, I was the mom shouting and cheering in the audience! We were all weeping! With Yeshua *all* things are possible! The road has been long and trying, but The Word of God stands *forever!*

Adi Tells Her Story:

"I'm afraid to grow up," I said to my dear grandfather. "You have your whole future in front of you," he said calmly. I was just a teenager. Not much later after that, my bed became my home. For a few months I couldn't get out of it -- clinical depression, anxieties... that was how my father died a few years before...

everything was dark and scary. And then... I found myself in bed, again... this time in a mental institution.

After I was doing a little better the doctors agreed to allow my mom to take me out of the hospital for a few hours. She took me to one of my favorite places – Office Depot. As a young child I loved school and that store was perfect for school supplies, but I was not smiling. I sat on the stairs of the store crying and crying, thinking about how my mom is wasting her money for me because I am just a waste... I will never ever study again.

A few years later, I was nearly turning twenty, and I was still in the hospital. The doctors said to my mother, "She will never recover and never have an intellect." It was true. I couldn't read nor write, couldn't calculate or use the English language.

My mom said as a response, "You do what you know to do, I will do what I know to do, and G-D will get her out of this."

A few weeks later, I was allowed to go out alone to the garden near the ward. Suddenly I felt the warm sun on my face and the light was strong, I smiled, and I was happy- the depression was gone! I was released and returned to school where I studied hard to complete my high school education. I used all the school supplies my mom bought for me that day. Now, I need to buy some more because... I'm doing my M.A in Special Education!

My Son Yuval

My son Yuval will also tell his own story below, but I will give you my side first. Yuval lost his father at the age of six. Yet his relationship with me was miraculously preserved to a degree. Maybe because he was so small they did not bother spending too much energy in alienating him from me or maybe because boys are sometimes more attached to their moms. However, he followed in the way of thinking of his dad's humanistic, existentialist upbringing and thus rejected the Faith in Messiah Yeshua. At the age of twelve he told me, *"I am inconvertible!"*

Of course, in the depths of my soul I heard the terrible echoes of his father's words prior to taking his life. The son was repeating the very same words that killed his father, *"I will never repent!"* And Yuval was only twelve!

My faith proclamation over his life overruled his words as I said with conviction, "You are not stronger than Elohim, you will become a believer!" I was basing my faith on a promise given to me by the God of Israel many years prior to this:

> "Restrain your voice from weeping and your eyes from tears; For your work will be rewarded," declares the Lord, "And they will return from the land of the enemy. There is hope for your future," declares the Lord, "And your children will return to their own territory."

> Jeremiah 31:16,17 NASB

However the road for Yuval's salvation would require every ounce of faith, courage and patience I could muster. I had to 'hang in there' with Yah's Promises in the face of all hopelessness and impossibility. My beloved husband and wonderful disciples and partners were praying for both of my children.

Yuval attempted suicide three times in the most violent of ways. In his last attempt, he actually succeeded in killing himself by cutting his own throat. He did this in the room next door to mine. I was awakened shortly before 4 AM by a phone call from my secretary who lived in the room adjacent to Yuval's.

Her dog, Halomi, was barking without ceasing and she could hear faint cries from my son's room. I got up at once and barged into his room only to find him half fainted on the bed surrounded by a pool of blood and the largest kitchen knife in the midst of it. I threw a blood curling cry into the air while trying to prevent my daughter, Adi, who woke up from the commotion, from seeing this horrific scene. Adi called the paramedics who were as shocked as we were to encounter such a violent scene. As Yuval was being wheeled on the stretcher to the ambulance he somehow managed to whisper, "Ima forgive me, I lied to you."

My husband Rabbi Baruch was doing a night shift as an armed guard that night, so he was not with us, but caught up with us at the hospital. Yuval was immediately taken to emergency surgery where, for the next four hours, doctors feverishly worked to save my son's life. As they did what they knew to do, my husband and I did what we knew to do – we declared the Word of God over Yuval focusing especially the following:

I will not die, but live, and tell of the works of the Lord.

Psalm 118:17

We proclaimed the Blood of the Covenant, which Yeshua our Messiah spilled on the cross for our sins, and the Promise that YHVH gave me about my children returning from the land of the enemy. As we declared the Word of YHVH and held on to

His promises, Adi struggled to overcome her desire to die in the midst of this. We held on to the promises for both my children.

When the surgeons came out they were pale. "Your son harmed himself very seriously," they said. Later on I asked the doctor, "Is it true that my son had one foot in this world and the other foot in the other world?" "No, Mrs. Bierman," he said, "Your son had *two feet in the other world.*"

Yuval was *dead*! But we continued proclaiming Yah's (God's) Word over him and we continued trusting His Promises and Covenant and Yuval was raised from the dead! This was not going to be the end.

I wish I could tell you that Yuval repented immediately and gave his life to Messiah. On the contrary, he was even more rebellious when he recovered and cut all ties with me and with his sister. After a drug episode, he was arrested and then admitted to the psychiatric hospital again – this time for nearly two years. For almost a year and a half he did not speak, and whenever we visited him, he would lie in bed with his face to the wall, his back toward us. During countless visits to the hospital I sat at the edge of his bed *singing prophetically* over his life. I prophesied the words and the plans of Yah for his life, even though there was no response to my actions for over a year and a half. I continued singing prophetically!

Upon release from the hospital, he was advised to go live in a psychiatric hostel, but I came up with another idea... We were willing to take Yuval to live in our Eilat Prayer Tower and give him a recovery program that would include studies and chores. At the same time, he would continue all psychiatric treatment.

Yuval was not very happy about this, but after a short visit to the psychiatric hostel, he decided to choose for 'the lesser of the two evils.' He joined our precious dedicated team of volunteers, to whom I will be forever grateful, in the Prayer Tower.

For nearly two years in the Tower, Yuval underwent a thorough 'mind wash' as he was required to study our GRM* video Bible School. He did not want this education but had no choice because he opted to come to the Prayer Tower. He also had to join the Team in prayer at 6 PM every day. Yuval graduated from our Bible School with honors, but *still in unbelief!* However, his character was changing, and he was becoming very respectful, loving and responsible.

Right before we closed the Eilat Prayer Tower (as the Year of Jubilee was starting), we saw a true transformation in Yuval as a result of Yah's faithful promises. This transformation lead to me having the enormous pleasure of leading my son to Yeshua. He was baptized in the waters of the Red Sea by his adoptive dad or "Pops" as he lovingly calls him, Rabbi Baruch. Today Yuval is on fire for Yeshua and has learned valuable lessons that are shaping his present and future.

His sister Adi, who has yet to surrender to the Messiah, is astonished at the change in her beloved brother. Every day I receive an email from Yuval – he sends me the special scriptures that spoke to his heart in his daily meditation of the Word of Yah (God). Often the Scriptures that he sends minister to me. Indeed my work is being rewarded as my son has returned from the land of the enemy. *My Elohim is faithful!*

---

* Global Revival MAP (Messianic Apostolic Prophetic)

Yuval Tells His Story

Suicide was a very relevant and sensitive topic in my early and adult life, but at the end of this testimony there is no death (as in a suicide), but only *life!*

Satan has been very active in my life and the life of my family in the form of mental illness. My late father was a manic-depressive non-believer. He killed himself twenty three years ago and some of his last words were, "I will never believe in God." I believe it is possible that this vow that my father made is what caused him to take his life.

Six years after my father committed suicide I was still a non-believer. Around age twelve, I was out with my mother and she was reading the Bible out loud. I felt ashamed and asked her to stop. She said, "A day will come when you will preach the Word with me." I told her, in a similar fashion to what my father said, "I am nonconvertible." Or in other words, "I will never believe."

I spent most of my life as a humanistic non-believer. I didn't understand the fact that my unbelief would be so costly, but it was very, very costly, so costly that I attempted suicide three times. I will share two of those times with you, as during and after the other one, I was so out of my mind that I cannot remember details.

At age 19, while serving in the Israeli military, I fell into a deep depression and consequently tried to take my own life, but I did not succeed. After 3 months in a mental hospital I was released, but not for long. Still a non-believer, 3 years later I fell into an even worse depression.

In this case I actually managed to kill myself and I was clinically dead on the operation table. My mother and stepfather prayed for Yeshua to raise me up from the dead and I rose. In this case I spent 9 months hospitalized, still putting my hope in psychiatry or psychology, not realizing the root issue was non-belief. Finally, I had a third breakdown that I did not believe I would recover from. I spent a whopping 2 years in the hospital! It appears that each time I was admitted to the hospital, I spent a longer time hospitalized.

Fortunately, the change came after my third and last hospitalization (The last, I proclaim in Yeshua's name!). My mother and stepfather accepted me into their Prayer Tower in the beautiful city of Eilat. I was still a non-believer but was 'forced' to join with others in prayer times and in their meetings. I was also obligated to complete my mother's GRM (Global Revival MAP) Bible School. I did not know that this was setting the foundation for me to become a believer.

Finally, after 28 years of unbelief I was transformed and decided it was time for me to become a believer and to be baptized and give my life to Yeshua! This was around the Day of Atonement in Israel, and I surely had many sins to atone for. Ever since then I have been a different person. My relationship with my family has never been better, and I am very stable mentally. I now believe in the following:

Surely your goodness and love will follow me all the days of my life, and I will dwell in the house of the Lord forever.

Psalm 23:6

I thank Yeshua and Yah for raising me from the dead, physically and mentally! And thanks to my mother and stepfather for leading me to be born again. I am certainly a testimony of 1 Corinthians 15:57:

But thanks be to God! He gives us the victory through our Lord Yeshua.

–Yuval

CHAPTER TWO

Suicide In the Bible

The Holy Bible is the most realistic book ever written. In the pages of what is commonly called the Old and New Testaments (the *Tanakh* and *Brit Chadasha*), you will find every one of the ills that plague society together with amazing acts of love and sacrifice. Because the Bible was written by real people inspired by the Spirit of Elohim (God) it gives us a very honest recount of the struggles of its heroes/heroines and anti-heroes. Therefore, the subject of suicide is mentioned several times and for various reasons. Suicide is found in the recounting of the stories of Samson and King Saul, Ahitophel - the Kingly advisor, and Judas Iscariot who betrayed Yeshua.

Samson – Suicide or an Act of Bravery?

And Samson said, "Let me die with the Philistines!" And he bent with all his might so that the house fell on the lords and all the people who were in it. So the dead whom he killed at his death were more than those whom he killed in his life.

Judges 16:30

It is hard to call Samson's death a pure act of suicide since he was fulfilling the purpose for which he was born. He was brought forth as an extraordinarily strong warrior and judge of Israel to take vengeance on the archenemy of Israel, the Philistines! However, he had a weakness for Philistine women and fell into immorality with a seductress called Delilah, which in Hebrew means 'thin and shallow with no substance.' Through his sin and trespass and after her painful nagging and probing, he confided the most important secret of his strength to this loose woman: as long as he did not shave his long hair (a sign of his dedication to The God of Israel as a Nazir*) he would have superhuman strength.

She shaved his hair while he was asleep, and the Philistines apprehended the weakened Samson. He lost his hair, the source of his strength as a Nazir unto YHVH (God) and the wicked Philistines also poked out his eyes making him blind. They used his suffering and humiliation as an object for their entertainment. Finally, when his hair began to grow, he found it in his heart to pray to the God who he had betrayed in order to satisfy his lustful appetite for foreign women. In the book of Judges we can read his prayer. This prayer changed the history of Israel, ended

---

* Nazir means consecrated in Hebrew. Samson was under a Nazirite vow which stipulates no consumption of grapes or grape products, unclean food or drink and a prohibition against cutting of the hair. See: Judges 13, Numbers 6

his life, and the lives of the most prominent personalities in the Philistine Stronghold of Gaza:

Then Samson called to the Lord and said, "O Lord [O] God, please remember me and please strengthen me just this time, O God, that I may at once be avenged of the Philistines for my two eyes." Samson grasped the two middle pillars on which the house rested, and braced himself against them, the one with his right hand and the other with his left. And Samson said, "Let me die with the Philistines!"

Judges 16:28-30

Elohim-God answered his prayer and he brought this Philistine temple down by a supernatural feat of power, killing about 3000 Philistines and dying as he requested. So he killed more enemies in his death than during his life.

What were Samson's motives? Were they hopelessness, depression, anger, revenge, fulfilling the purpose for which he was born? Was it the judgment of God? Why did God answer his prayer to die with the Philistines? Can this qualify as a normal suicide? (As if there is anything "normal" about suicide.)

In my eyes this was not a "normal" suicide, but rather an act of desperate bravery and revenge. The situation of Samson was hopeless. He had forfeited his mission by falling into sin and immorality. The Word of God says that the wages of sin is death. He changed the course of events when he went to bed with the Philistine Delilah. The outcome of this was a devastating bondage and yet in the midst of this he found it in his heart not to preserve his life, but rather to lose his life in order to give Israel the victory against their enemies.

He fulfilled Yah's calling to defeat the Philistines, and avenged himself as well, for his two blinded eyes.

Samson made it right after doing wrong. He forfeited his God-given mission because he loved his life and his lust for women, but he fulfilled his mission by losing his life for a higher purpose. We will notice that in most modern day cases of suicide, those who kill themselves do not have a vision or a higher purpose in mind. For the most part, they hear voices in their mind who tell them that the only way to alleviate their suffering is to kill themselves. These voices are demonic spirits speaking into the minds of individuals. Samson did not turn to Satan, but to YHVH to give him supernatural strength to fulfill his mission and take revenge on his enemies – thus he became a hero.

I am not here assessing the morality of his death, but only shedding light on his motives. Those who kill themselves to fulfill a mission or to save others have a very different mind than those who kill themselves because they have decided to turn away from God or because they do not see another solution. No human could have broken these massive stone pillars. This was An Act of The Almighty. Samson's name and ministry were redeemed. His humiliation was turned into an act of bravery and victory for Israel.

King Saul – Suicide as an Act of Honor

Then Saul said to his armor bearer, "Draw your sword and thrust me through with it, otherwise these uncircumcised will come and abuse me.", but his armor bearer would not, for he was greatly afraid. Therefore Saul took his sword and fell on it.

1 Chronicles 10:4

In ancient times it was customary for a great warrior or king to kill himself rather than to fall into the hands of his enemies. King Saul had lost the battle against the Philistines on Mount Gilboa in the North of Israel. His sons also lost their lives in this battle and, of course, through this loss Saul lost all dignity – only torment was awaiting him from his cruel captors and a sure death at their hands. He did that which seemed like the lesser of the two evils. What was customary in the ancient world was that either the armor bearer would end his life, or the king would do it himself.

In this case the armor bearer refused to lay his hands on his king, so Saul had to do it himself. The armor bearer followed suit as an act of loyalty and killed himself as well. With the death of his King, his life's purpose as an armor bearer and protector to the king had ended.

When his armor bearer saw that Saul was dead, he likewise fell on his sword and died. Thus Saul died with his three sons, and all those of his house died together.

1 Chronicles 10:5,6

The case of this suicide was more cultural than a desperate act of depression. Of course, terrible disappointment, failure and fear affected Saul's decision, but in his day and time this was the customary thing to do in order to avoid the humiliation of being tormented by the vanquishing enemy. The armor bearer's act was an act of loyalty to the king, not of betrayal.

Again I am not assessing the morality of this, but rather detecting the frame of mind these two men were in when they decided to take their lives. Theirs's was a very different frame of mind than most of the modern day suicides.' We also must remember that Saul had turned away from following The God of Israel and had betrayed his royal calling much earlier. His defeat on Mt. Gilboa was an Act of Judgment that would transfer the Kingdom to the Chosen King, David, as prophesied by Samuel the Prophet.

> *So Samuel said to him, "The Lord has torn the kingdom of Israel from you today and has given it to your neighbor, who is better than you."*

> 1 Samuel 15:28

Ultimately Saul's tragic defeat and death was the outcome of his disobedience to The Almighty which caused him to be possessed of spirits of jealousy and anger. He persecuted his son-in-law, David, for many years though David had nothing against him. Saul was crazy with jealousy because David was favored by YHVH to become the next king in his place.

> *Then Samuel took the horn of oil and anointed him in the midst of his brothers; and the Spirit of Adonai came*

mightily upon David from that day forward. And Samuel arose and went to Ramah. Now the Spirit of Adonai departed from Saul, and an evil spirit from the Lord terrorized him. Saul's servants then said to him, "Behold now, an evil spirit from God is terrorizing you."

1 Samuel 16:13-15

The Holy Spirit departed from Saul and evil spirits began to torment Saul. Many people are tormented by evil spirits because of compromise, rebellion, immorality, idolatry and unforgiveness. Saul lost all of his ability to conquer when he turned his back on YHVH. The battle on Mount Gilboa was the outcome of his rebellion and the reason for his untimely death.

Saul was a bad loser and later on we will see that disobedience to God's call, bitterness and jealousy can cause serious mental problems and even lead to untimely death.

Ahithophel – Suicide as a Response to Offended Pride

Now when Ahithophel saw that his counsel was not followed, he saddled his donkey and arose and went to his home, to his city, and set his house in order, and strangled himself; thus he died and was buried in the grave of his father.

2 Samuel 17:23

Ahithophels' professional pride killed him! He had been the advisor to King David prior to the takeover of Absalom, his son, who usurped the Kingdom of Israel from his father. When David fled from his son Absalom, Achithophel stayed in Jerusalem to serve under the traitor son. He was a man with no scruples and did not fear YHVH at all. In fact, he advised the usurper Absalom to lie with the concubines of his father on the roof so all of Israel could see how the son was defying and defiling his father.

> Then Absalom said to Ahithophel, "Give your advice. What shall we do?" Ahithophel said to Absalom, "Go in to your father's concubines, whom he has left to keep the house; then all Israel will hear that you have made yourself odious to your father. The hands of all who are with you will also be strengthened." So they pitched a tent for Absalom on the roof, and Absalom went in to his father's concubines in the sight of all Israel. The advice of Ahithophel, which he gave in those days, was as if one inquired of the word of God; so was all the advice of Ahithophel regarded by both David and Absalom.
>
> 1 Kings 16:20-23

Ahithophel was simply wicked, selfish and ambitious. He did not care about what was right or wrong as long as it served his self -ambitious agenda. He lived for himself and loved to be appreciated for his "professionalism" and talents.

Later on he gave other advice to Absalom that was rejected in favor of the advice of a wise man who was working on David's behalf to defeat the wayward son Absalom. When Ahithophel saw that he had lost his *status* as the infallible advisor, his pride was so hurt that he could not tolerate living anymore. He lived only for his 'professional pride.' He did not live for God or love or anything else, so when his 'professional pride' was removed, he took his life.

How many people, when they fail in their business or lose money, status or fame, prefer to die rather than face a life without them? How many prefer death to shame or losing face? Probably many, but I have great news! When a person humbles himself before The God of Heaven and Earth to *repent*, he can find forgiveness, grace and life! That is why Yeshua died, so he can make us free to live, not for ourselves, but for Him.

Let the wicked forsake his way and the unrighteous man his thoughts; and let him return to the Lord, And He will have compassion on him, And to our God, For He will abundantly pardon.

Isaiah 55:7

When you live for yourself, sooner or later you will experience failure or loss of dignity, as all us humans do, at a certain point. It is at this point we must choose: will pride lead us to hopelessness and suicide because of the emptiness of a self-centered life, or will we humble ourselves and receive the salvation of our souls and lives through the name of Yeshua, the Jewish Messiah who paid the price so we could *live*?

Humble yourselves in the presence of the Lord, and He will exalt you.

Yaakov (James) 4:10

Elijah – The Great Prophet Who Wanted to Die

*But he himself went a day's journey into the wilderness, and
came and sat down under a juniper tree; and he requested
for himself that he might die, and said, "It is enough; now,
O Lord, take my life, for I am not better than my fathers."*

1 Kings 19:4

Elijah was the most powerful Prophet of his time and for all
generations. He accomplished no small feat when he convened
all of Israel to Mt. Carmel together with all the false prophets of
the pagan gods baal and ashera (Ishtar or Easter). The Northern
Kingdom of Israel was in terrible idolatry, ruled by a puppet king
called Ahab and a wicked witch of a woman, a Sidonian, who
was the high priestess of the goddess of fertility, ashera or Ishtar.

Due to idolatry which brought on Elijah's declaration that it
would not rain, there was a terrible drought in the land (1 Kings
17). In order to avert this judgment that was causing a deathly
famine there was a need for *repentance*. However the people
were trapped in this idolatrous system headed by the king and
the queen and they would not repent unless The God of Israel
would reveal Himself as the One True God.

Elijah contested the idolatrous system as he demanded
a sacrifice to God on Mt. Carmel in Northern Israel. He told
all the ones who were worshipping the foreign idols to make a
sacrifice to their god and Elijah would make a sacrifice to his
God, YHVH, The God of Israel. During this contest, the God
of Israel would answer with *fire* from above, thereby proving that
He is the True God! This was a supernatural test as Elijah was

certain that Elohim would back him up, which indeed he did! (1 Kings 18)

For an entire day all the priests of baal and ashera cried out to their idols and cut themselves with stones with absolutely no answer from above. Yet when Elijah presented his sacrifice before sunset, YHVH rained fire from Heaven, which consumed the animal offering and the water in the trenches around it, leaving nothing that the fire did not consume. This provoked repentance as the fear of God fell on the people.

> *Answer me, O YHVH, answer me, that this people may know that You, O YHVH, are God, and that You have turned their heart back again." Then the fire of the Lord fell and consumed the burnt offering and the wood and the stones and the dust and licked up the water that was in the trench. When all the people saw it, they fell on their faces; and they said, "YHVH, He is God; YHVH, He is God."*
>
> 1 Kings 18:37-39

Then Elijah proceeded to single handedly kill 850 false prophets by his own hand. As if this would have not been enough, he also went to the summit of Mt. Carmel to pray and interceded until rain would come. When a cloud showed up in the sky, an omen that rain was coming, Elijah outran King Ahab's chariot!

> *In a little while the sky grew black with clouds and wind, and there was a heavy shower. And Ahab rode and went to*

Jezreel. Then the hand of the Lord was on Elijah, and he girded up his loins and outran Ahab to Jezreel.

1 Kings 18:45,46

What a *day* for Elijah and for all of Israel! Yet when it was all over and the Prophet was completely spent and exhausted, the wicked Queen Jezebel sent death threats of intimidation. At this point Elijah was not ready for such an intense emotional battle. This Amazing Man of Yah (God), who killed the 850 false prophets single handedly and outran Ahab's chariot, now stood vulnerable and in fear of Jezebel -- so *he prayed to die.*

Was Elijah in general "suicidal" or the "depressive type?" Of course not, but after great victories that demand both spiritual, emotional and physical expenditure, the enemy comes, as is his custom, to attack us in our moments of weakness. A man or woman of God needs to be wise, seeking shelter and *rest*. People of Great Spiritual Stature like Elijah, and those of us in the Ministry, are only flesh and blood. Once the Mission is over and the Anointing subsides we need to 'hide' and rest.

Are you in Ministry or in any kind of executive position that demands everything you are in order to fulfill your role? Once you finish the assignment, you need to take time off and replenish, physically (rest and food), emotionally (rest and recreation) and Spiritually (quiet prayer, meditation on His Word, worship and thanksgiving, but in an attitude of resting in His Presence).

Warning- Do not go from mission to mission, assignment to assignment without a time of R&R in between. Do not face any more challenges or enemies. When you are done *just rest*! This will protect you from depression and collapse due to exhaustion.

> *He lay down and slept under a juniper tree; and behold, there was an angel touching him, and he said to him, "Arise, eat." Then he looked and behold, there was at his head a bread cake baked on hot stones, and a jar of water. So he ate and drank and lay down again. The angel of the Lord came again a second time and touched him and said, "Arise, eat, because the journey is too great for you." So he arose and ate and drank and went in the strength of that food forty days and forty nights to Horeb,the mountain of God.*

1 Kings 18:5-8

Judas – Suicide as the Ultimate Act of Betrayal

> *Then when Judas, who had betrayed Him, saw that He had been condemned, he felt remorse and returned the thirty pieces of silver to the chief priests and elders, saying, "I have sinned by betraying innocent blood." But they said, "What is that to us? See to that yourself!" And he threw the pieces of silver into the temple sanctuary and departed; and he went away and hanged himself.*

Matthew 27:3-5

The story of Judas gives a clear answer as to why people who call themselves believers or Christians can also fall prey to Satan and commit suicide. Judas had walked, lived and served with Yeshua for three and a half years. He was one of the Chosen Twelve and he was entrusted with the treasury, unfortunately he was a thief!

Mary then took a pound of very costly perfume of pure nard and anointed the feet of Yeshua and wiped His feet with her hair; and the house was filled with the fragrance of the perfume., but Judas Iscariot, one of His disciples, who was intending to betray Him, said, "Why was this perfume not sold for three hundred denarii and given to poor people?" Now he said this, not because he was concerned about the poor, but because he was a thief, and as he had the money box, he used to pilfer what was put into it.

John 12:3-6

Among the Top Twelve Disciples, Judas was the most religious, sanctimonious and self-righteous. He was also probably the most knowledgeable in the Scriptures and had connections with the religious leadership in high places. That is why he was entrusted with the dirty job of betraying the Messiah. However, he did not do this for the love of God, but rather, for the love of money. He got paid for his *job* of betrayal. His god was *Mammon*!

Then one of the twelve, named Judas Iscariot, went to the chief priests and said, "What are you willing to give me to betray Him to you?" And they weighed out thirty pieces of silver to him. From then on he began looking for a good opportunity to betray Yeshua.

Matthew 26:14-16

Whether you are a Christian, a Messianic Jew or profess no religion, if money is your god expect terrible things to happen in your life. This is one of the most common causes of depression and suicidal desires among all people, but especially the believers. When you know God's Commandments and what pleases Him, and yet, because of your *job*, you disobey Him, you are setting yourself up for death and destruction! This includes when you choose to work for your money on the Sabbath that He set apart as holy unto Him.

Observe the sabbath day to keep it holy, as the Lord your God commanded you. Six days you shall labor and do all your work, but the seventh day is a sabbath of the Lord your God; in it you shall not do any work, you or your son or your daughter or your male servant or your female servant or your ox or your donkey or any of your cattle or your sojourner who stays with you, so that your male servant and your female servant may rest as well as you. You shall remember that you were a slave in the land of Egypt, and the Lord your God brought you out of there by a mighty hand and by an outstretched arm; therefore the Lord your God commanded you to observe the sabbath day.

Deuteronomy 5:12-15

Most people in the Church are exhausted from pursuing elusive money and they hardly give Yeshua any time at all. They do not have time for prayer or meditation in the Word – and since so many do not honor this one day of *rest* a week, they can hardly keep their spiritual lives together.

This is a ticket for disaster. Money is not the problem – it is the love of money that is the root of all evil. YHVH wants us to prosper, but not at the expense of our relationship with Him, with His People and with our families. A great repentance is needed in this area! Far too many Christians go to church for an hour or two a week and then they forget about their spiritual lives. Money takes center stage, and this is detrimental, putting believers in grave danger.

> *But those who want to get rich fall into temptation and a snare and many foolish and harmful desires which plunge men into ruin and destruction. For the love of money is a root of all sorts of evil, and some by longing for it have wandered away from the faith and pierced themselves with many griefs.*
>
> 1 Timothy 6:9,10

Notice these words: Pierced themselves with many griefs!

This is a most graphic picture of depression and suicide. So many Christians are piercing themselves (yes, even body piercing) or slitting their wrists or inflicting other physical harm to themselves. And why? Because of idolatry. Any time we put anything or anyone above our love for Elohim-God through Messiah Yeshua, we will experience grief, depression and ultimately even suicide.

Judas Iscariot 'went to church' and even served on the leadership team of Messiah, but his heart was divided. He had selfish agendas and did not know his Rabbi-Pastor – he did not know the Lord. "Knowing" in Hebrew is the word YADA which is the same word to describe intimacy between husband and wife. You can go to church, even serve – yes, even cast out demons or prophesy –, but you may not truly *know* Him. To know Him always leads to obedience and placing Him at the center of your life, thoughts and speech. The Bible warns us that there are many church-goers who will not enter into Eternal Life:

"Not everyone who says to Me, 'Lord, Lord,' will enter the kingdom of heaven, but he who does the will of My Father who is in heaven will enter. Many will say to Me on that day, 'Lord, Lord, did we not prophesy in Your name, and in Your name cast out demons, and in Your name perform many miracles?' And then I will declare to them, 'I never knew you; depart from Me, you who practice lawlessness.'

Matthew 7:21-23

The betrayal of Judas started way before he gave Yeshua over to the religious authorities. It started when his heart was attached to money and his own agenda rather than to a pure devotion to Messiah. His ultimate betrayal was the act of suicide: he hanged himself after he had experienced remorse over his act. If he had known the Messiah even a little, he would have *repented* instead of killing himself, but Judas, through his idolatry and self-righteous pride, was so disconnected from the love of Yah (God) that he did not even find it in his heart to cry out for mercy. Yeshua made provision for Judas' repentance when hanging on the Cross he said:

> *Father forgive them (all his executors and betrayers) for they do not know what they do.*

Luke 23:34

Alas! Judas had no faith in the amazing compassion and goodness of Elohim! And he was too prideful and religious to *repent* and ask for mercy. Had he done that he would have been forgiven and history would have been very different.

> *YHVH is compassionate and gracious, Slow to anger and abounding in lovingkindness. He will not always strive with us, nor will He keep His anger forever. He has not dealt with us according to our sins, nor rewarded us according to our iniquities. For as high as the heavens are above the earth, so great is His lovingkindness toward those who fear Him. As far as the east is from the west, so far has He removed our transgressions from us. Just as a father has compassion on his children, So YHVH has compassion on those who fear Him. For He Himself knows our frame; He is mindful that we are, but dust.*

Psalm 103:8-14

If you are a believer/Christian/Messianic and you are suffering from depression and suicide TURN TO YESHUA.

Do not run away from Him. There is nothing that He cannot forgive if you turn to Him. Repent of your sins, of any way that you have loved something or someone above Him, especially if your job and money have been your god.

Receive forgiveness by faith as you choose to forsake old ways that are ungodly. Hold onto your faith for dear life and begin to proclaim His Word over all the demonic voices that you hear in your mind. Do not forget to forgive all others who have wronged you! Especially if they do not deserve your forgiveness – remember, none of us deserves it! Keep your heart *pure*, ask for forgiveness, receive His forgiveness and *give* forgiveness!

> *Whenever you stand praying, forgive, if you have anything against anyone, so that your Father who is in heaven will also forgive you your transgressions.*

> Mark 11:25

Look at this powerful promise that you can stand on. By holding on to this promise, you can be cleansed from all evil including suicidal thoughts:

> *If we say that we have fellowship with Him and yet walk in the darkness, we lie and do not practice the truth; but if we walk in the Light as He Himself is in the Light, we have fellowship with one another, and the blood of Yeshua His Son cleanses us from all sin. If we say that we have no sin, we are deceiving ourselves and the truth is not in us. If we*

confess our sins, He is faithful and righteous to forgive us our sins and to cleanse us from all unrighteousness.

1 John 1:6-9

When we turn to Him and seek Him, we get supernatural help from The Father – be assured deliverance is on its way! Do not lose hope! Call someone who walks with God to pray with you to increase your strength.

In Hebrew the word *repentance* is *teshuva*, which means:

Returning (to God) for the purpose of restoration. It implies believing that He is *good, merciful* and *forgiving*! It also means *the answer*. The answer to all the woes of mankind including depression and suicide is teshuva. In order to do teshuva we must humble ourselves and pray.

If My people who are called by My name humble themselves and pray and seek My face and turn from their wicked ways, then I will hear from heaven, will forgive their sin and will heal their land.

2 Chronicles 7:14

Our land includes our physical bodies (made out of earth) and our soul, emotions and mind. All that 'territory' can be healed *if* we humble ourselves, pray, seek Him and turn – which means *TESHUVA, returning for the purpose of restoration*!

Judas Iscariot's ultimate betrayal was suicide as he did not do *teshuva*, but you, in this moment, can do teshuva and *live*!

The thief comes only to steal and kill and destroy; I came that they may have life and have it abundantly.

John 10:10

Abundant life is yours through *teshuva*, not eternal destruction through suicide. *Choose life*!

CHAPTER THREE

Exposing Existentialism

This book of the law shall not depart from your mouth,
but you shall meditate on it day and night, so that you
may be careful to do according to all that is written in it;
for then you will make your way prosperous, and then you
will have success.

Joshua 1:8

The Religion of Unbelief & Restoring a Healthy Logic

Logic in Hebrew is *higayon*, which means "meditation." A healthy logic meditates on Elohim's Word and Promises -- a sick logic meditates on personal suffering and experience. In a healthy logic YHVH and His Truth are in the Center, whereas in sick logic the human being and his suffering are in the center. Modern day psychology, which is rooted in Existential Humanism or "sickology", is a Sick Logic that causes more unbelief, depression, suicide and death than anything else. Elohim-God destroyed the Noah Generation via a flood because their thinking was evil leading to evil deeds!

> *Then YHVH saw that the wickedness of man was great on the earth, and that* every intent of the thoughts of his heart was only evil continually. *The Lord was sorry that He had made man on the earth, and He was grieved in His heart.*
>
> Genesis 6:5,6

What we think about becomes an action and our way of life. Humanistic Psychology is the 'logic' of the Snake!

> *Now the serpent was more crafty than any beast of the field which the Lord God had made. And he said to the woman, "Indeed, has Elohim said, 'You shall not eat from any tree of the garden'?"*
>
> Genesis 3:1

The word *logic* comes from the Greek word *logos*, which means "the *word.*" On what word you meditate determines if you will be whole or sick in your 'logic' or thinking mind. The snake in the Garden of Eden convinced the Woman to trust the snake's logic or the snake's word, which said that Elohim did not care about them enough to let them eat of the Death Tree of Knowledge of Good and Evil.

*The serpent said to the woman, "You surely will not die!
For God knows that in the day you eat from it your eyes
will be opened, and you will be like God, knowing good
and evil.*

Genesis 3:4,5

When she trusted in the snake's logical argument and deductions rather than in the *logos* of Elohim, she broke His Commandment. As a result, she and her husband died spiritually, and eventually physically, in less than 1,000 years, which is like a Day unto YHVH.

*But from the tree of the knowledge of good and evil you
shall not eat, for in the day that you eat from it you will
surely die."*

Genesis 2:17

The reality of *Adam* became the reality of the *curse*. Ever since the garden, men seek to explain that reality with snake's logic of existentialism and humanism rather than with the LOGOS, which explains the Fall of Man as the cause of the curse.

There is no way out of the curse through philosophy or any human act, and therefore the philosophy of nihilism says that everything is meaningless. That is why the Book of Job and Ecclesiastes are so popular with Jewish Existential Philosophers starting with Franz Kafka and continuing all the way to Rabbi Nachman from Braslev. From this philosophy that everything is meaningless, the Psychology of suffering comes into being and the impact of existentialism can be seen in its influence of Freud and modern day psychology and psychiatry.

Existentialism

Existentialism– Philosophical movement centered on individual existence: a philosophical movement begun in the 19th century that denies that the universe has any intrinsic meaning or purpose.*

> Existentialism is a term applied to the work of certain late 19th- and 20th-century philosophers who, despite profound doctrinal differences shared the belief that philosophical thinking begins with the human subject—not merely the thinking subject, but the acting, feeling, living human individual. In existentialism, the individual's starting point is characterized by what has been called "the existential attitude", or a sense of disorientation and confusion in the face of an apparently meaningless or absurd world.**

> Most of modern day Judaism (contrary to Biblical Judaism) and existentialism, deny the ability of human beings to permanently transcend the physical world and one's own normal existence. Theistic Judaism insists on a transcendent realm of existence beyond normal human reality, that is, the realm of God. As a way of connecting to God, Judaism directs its adherents towards the strict

---

* (Microsoft® Encarta® 2009. © 1993-2008 Microsoft Corporation. All rights reserved.)

** (wikipedia.org/wiki/Existentialism, Accessed 22 Sept. 2016)

observance of laws,

both ritual and ethical, in order to add meaning to the adherents' lives (see Soloveitchik's Halakhic Man for a further discussion of the concept of the Jew making meaning in his own life by observing the Halakha).[*]

Modern existentialist philosophy often denies the existence of a higher power, leading some to classify it as an agnostic or atheistic thought structure. Martin Heidegger's concept of man's thrownness into existence in the world causing him to be ill at ease/ uncomfortable due to his very existence is similar to Hebraic man's "uneasiness" due to his inherently sinful nature. Both senses of being ill at ease in one's own skin are too inherent to the human condition to eliminate, according to Barret. Traditional Jewish thinkers and existentialist thinkers (both Semitic and gentile) have different solutions to this intrinsic uneasiness, also called existential anxiety or existential angst.[**]

Jewish existentialism is a category of work by Jewish authors dealing with existentialist themes and concepts (e.g. debate about the existence of God and the meaning of human existence) and is intended to answer theological questions that are important in Judaism. The existential angst of Job is an example from the Hebrew Bible of the existentialist theme.

---

[*]   (wikipedia.org/wiki/Jewish_existentialism, Accessed 22 Sept. 2016)

[**]   ibid

Theodicy and post-Holocaust theology make up a large part of 20th century Jewish existentialism. [*]

Jewish Existentialism Is Hitler's "Child"

Jewish Existentialism became a movement after the horrors of the Shoa (Holocaust). Many Jews grew disappointed and angry with God and denied His existence or tried to find religious explanations misinterpreting the Word of God.

But realize this, that in the last days difficult times will come. For men will be lovers of self, lovers of money, boastful, arrogant, revilers, disobedient to parents, ungrateful, unholy, unloving, irreconcilable, malicious gossips, without self-control, brutal, haters of good, treacherous, reckless, conceited, lovers of pleasure rather than lovers of God, holding to a form of godliness, although they have denied its power.

2 Timothy 3:1-5

Jewish existentialism finds its roots in both the traditional philosophical school of existentialism and the peculiarities of modern day Jewish theology, Biblical commentary, and European Jewish culture. Existentialism, as a philosophical system, grew as a result of the works of such non-Jewish thinkers as Søren Kierkegaard, Friedrich Nietzsche, Albert Camus, and

---

[*]   wikipedia.org/wiki/Jewish existentialism, Accessed 22 Sept. 2016 ibid

Martin Heidegger.[*]

The Books of Ecclesiastes and Job, found in the Hebrew Bible and often cited as examples of wisdom literature in the Hebrew Biblical tradition, include existentialist themes. The Book of Job tells the story of Job, who is beset by both God and Satan with many hardships intended to test his faith. He ultimately keeps his faith and receives redemption and rewards from God. The Book of Job includes many discussions between Job and his friends, as well as between Job and God concerning the nature, origin, and purpose of evil and suffering in the world.[**]

The Book of Ecclesiastes is broader in scope and includes many meditations on the meaning of life and God's purpose for human beings on Earth. Passages in Ecclesiastes describe human existence in such terms as "all is futile" and "futile and pursuit of wind."

Much Biblical scholarship and Talmud exegesis has been devoted to exploring the apparent contradiction between the affirmation of an all-powerful God's existence and the futility, meaningless, and/or difficulty of human life. Judaism's treatment of theodicy makes heavy use of the Books of Job and Ecclesiastes.[***]

---

[*]   (wikipedia.org/wiki/Jewish_existentialism, Accessed 22 Sept. 2016)
[**]   ibid
[***]   (wikipedia.org/wiki/Jewish_existentialism, Accessed 22 Sept. 2016)

The Mistaken Starting Point

Whether Gentile existentialists, Jewish secular existentialists (Franz Kafka) or Jewish religious existentialists (like Rabbi Nachman from Braslev), they all have a common concept: man's reality is the starting point. It is from man's reality and personal experience that one has the right to design his own beliefs or disbeliefs about life. They all negate the need for redemption *outside* of themselves. They do not acknowledge the need for the Act of Redemption of Yeshua (Jesus) on the Cross. In the eyes of all existentialists, they deserve happiness. Any way that they pursue this happiness, based on their own reality, belief system and experience, is valid.

"In the beginning God created the heavens and the earth" Genesis 1:1 is replaced with 'in the beginning *man* creates his own world according to his own reality and experience!'

> *All of us like sheep have gone astray, each of us has turned to his own way;, but YHVH has caused the iniquity of us all to fall on Him.*
>
> Isaiah 53:6

Get around God (secular) or get *up* to God (religious) by our own strength, as man did in Genesis 11. Both are existential-humanistic theologies that deny the Truth of God's Word that says:

> *For the wages of sin is death, but the free gift of God is eternal life in Messiah Yeshua our Lord.*
>
> Romans 6:23

When the starting point of life's philosophy is self, the end is hell, both in this life and in the life to come. Being self-centered is *pride* against the Creator and His Laws.

But He gives a greater grace. Therefore it says, "God is opposed to the proud, but gives grace to the humble." Submit therefore to God. Resist the devil and he will flee from you.

Yaakov (James) 4:6,7

Psychology Comes to the "Rescue"?

Since man cannot transcend the reality of the curse by his own means, psychological treatment and psychiatric medications will assist him in coping with this reality. This psychological philosophy even gives validation to suicide, seeing it only as a 'fair attempt' of human beings to escape the suffering by harming themselves. In that sense, a person who tries to commit suicide should have no guilt at all, because he is just doing the 'existential thing' of coming out of his own pain and suffering and finding a solution that matches his reality of depression and despair. Thus, repentance from sin has no entrance in modern day Psychology. Therefore, drugs and analysis take the place of TESHUVA (*Repentance*), returning to Elohim and His ways, and so Psychiatry takes the place of God.

Or do you not know that your body is a temple of the Holy Spirit who is in you, whom you have from God, and that you are not your own? For you have been bought with a price: therefore glorify God in your body.

1 Corinthians 6:19,20

Suicide is self-murder and it is a crime against the Creator, not only against oneself. Psychiatry says it is not a crime because it is only harming oneself in order to come out of pain, taking no regards for the laws of God, and in fact repudiating them while making the psychiatrist to be as "god." Thus, now the god-psychiatrist will prescribe heavy drugs in an attempt to alter the mind of the individual to prevent him from alleviating his suffering by harming or killing himself.

Repentance Leads to Freedom

If My people who are called by My name humble themselves and pray and seek My face and turn from their wicked ways, then I will hear from heaven, will forgive their sin and will heal their land.

2 Chronicles 7:14

Repentance would lead the "sufferer" into *freedom*, the freedom of encountering God's forgiveness for his sin through the sacrifice of the Blood of Yeshua. Psychiatry instead leads the "sufferer" into bondage, the bondage to the religion of existentialism, and through it to drugs that should be illicit! More people kill themselves *after* they start drug treatment, but it has been excused by the fact that the sufferers came to the psychiatrist because they were sick. Interestingly enough, going through the suffering and seeking God in the midst of that suffering has never killed anybody, but taking psychiatric drugs has and very often does.

Job went through his suffering, seeking God for 40 chapters as he vented his hurt feelings before the Creator of Life, thinking to himself that he was more righteous and more wise than God. In the 41st Chapter, Elohim speaks for the first time since Job's suffering began, and He said, "Who do you think you are Job?" In other words your logic is not my logic. Your thoughts are not My thoughts! And what counts are not your thoughts, but MY thoughts. "I created you, remember?"

In Existentialism and Psychology, what counts are *man's* thoughts, and it totally discounts the Thoughts of the Creator of *life*! Below is His instruction for wellbeing; His Word is the *source* and starting point!

Seek YHVH while He may be found; Call upon Him while He is near. Let the wicked forsake his way and the unrighteous man his thoughts; and let him return to YHVH and He will have compassion on him, and to our God, for He will abundantly pardon."For My thoughts are not your thoughts, nor are your ways My ways," declares the Lord. "For as the heavens are higher than the earth, so are My ways higher than your ways and My thoughts than your thoughts. "For as the rain and the snow come down from heaven, and do not return there without watering the earth and making it bear and sprout, and furnishing seed to the sower and bread to the eater; So will My word be which goes forth from My mouth; It will not return to Me empty, without accomplishing what I desire, and without succeeding in the matter for which I sent it. "For you will go out with joy and be led forth with peace; the mountains and the hills will break forth into shouts of joy before you, and all the trees of the field will clap their hands. "Instead of the thorn bush the cypress will come up, and instead of the nettle the myrtle will come up, and it will be a memorial to YHVH, for an everlasting sign which will not be cut off."

Isaiah 55:6-13

CHAPTER FOUR

The Futility of Life?

When King Solomon said that *all* is *futile*, he meant all of man's quest for knowledge according to the Death Tree of knowledge of good and evil is futile; in other words he was condemning existentialism and humanism and he summarized it this way:

The conclusion, when all has been heard, is: fear God and keep His commandments, because this applies to every person.

Ecclesiastes 12:13

Jews and Gentiles who rejected salvation through the Blood Sacrifice of the Innocent Lamb of God -- Yeshua the Messiah -- have attempted to escape the curse through religion. They recognize the condition but have concocted a cure of their own that does not need the intervention of Elohim through the Blood on the Altar. There is no need for redemptive blood when "good works" (*mitzvot* in Hebrew) become the atonement for sin, but the Word is clear, that *only* the blood of a sinless animal can atone for sin. However YHVH goes further to say, "I have given it to you on the altar..."

> *For the life of the flesh is in the blood, and I have given it to you on the altar to make atonement for your souls; for it is the blood by reason of the life that makes atonement.'*

Leviticus 17:11

He gave us His Blood through His Son Yeshua on the Altar just as clearly described in Isaiah Chapter 53:

> *Surely our griefs He Himself bore, and our sorrows He carried; yet we ourselves esteemed Him stricken, smitten of God, and afflicted. But He was pierced through for our transgressions, He was crushed for our iniquities; the chastening for our well-being (shalom) fell upon Him, and by His scourging we are healed. All of us like sheep have gone astray, each of us has turned to his own way;, but YHVH has caused the iniquity of us all to fall on Him. He was oppressed and He was afflicted, yet He did not open His mouth; like a lamb that is led to slaughter. He was cut off out of the land of the living for the transgression of my people, to whom the stroke was due? But YHVH was pleased to crush Him, putting Him to grief; If He would render Himself as a guilt offering because He poured out Himself to death, and was numbered with the transgressors; and interceded for the transgressors.*

Isaiah 53:4-7, 8, 10, 12

The difference between faith in a Living God (who is compassionate and redeems Mankind though we did not deserve it) and Jewish Religious Existentialism is that Existentialism claims that we (Jews) are all Holy and Righteous (Zadikim) by the mere fact that we are Jews. Therefore, we do not need Yeshua or Salvation, or any mediator, to rescue us from our sins, but, rather, "good works" or mitsvot.

For a believer in Messiah the 'good works' follow the Act of Redemption but does not precede it. There is nothing that we can do to save our lives from the coming judgment of Elohim. Nothing can redeem us from the curse of the law besides the Holy Blood of the Sinless Lamb of God. The mark of true faith in Yeshua and of true salvation is the Torah written on the heart of the believer; thus the response to Salvation is acts of obedience based on faith, but it cannot precede it. The Blood of the New Covenant precedes it!

> *"Behold, days are coming," declares YHVH, "when I will make a new covenant with the house of Israel and with the house of Judah, not like the covenant which I made with their fathers in the day I took them by the hand to bring them out of the land of Egypt, My covenant which they broke, although I was a husband to them," declares the Lord. "But this is the covenant which I will make with the house of Israel after those days," declares the Lord, "I will put My law within them and on their heart I will write it; and I will be their God, and they shall be My people. They will not teach again, each man his neighbor and each man his brother, saying, 'Know the Lord,' for they will all know*

> *Me, from the least of them to the greatest of them," declares
> the Lord, "for I will forgive their iniquity, and their sin I
> will remember no more."*

Jeremiah 31:31-34

The Fruit of Psychology & Existentialism

Existentialism and psychology is a placebo or a band-aid for
the cancer of rebellion and unbelief in the Creator of Life. It
eventually bears fruit: more hopelessness, confusion, despair
through self- centeredness and selfishness leading to suicide,
murder and the like. Why? Because *man* is in the center and
nothing is a matter of *conscience*, but rather of *personal feeling*:
"If it feels good do it." It does not matter if we 'hurt the feelings'
of the Creator by breaking His Commandments. What matters
is that we do not hurt our own human feelings!

> *For they exchanged the truth of God for a lie and worshiped
> and served the creature rather than the Creator, who is
> blessed forever. Amen.*

Romans 1:25

Psychology and Existentialism is a *spirit*. All theology and
words come with a spirit. Both the words and the spirit of
Existential Humanism and Psychology must be exposed to the
light and defeated so that people can be set *free*!

There are many researches who prove that most people
commit suicide after they start taking psychiatric drugs.
There is a direct relationship between psychology, psychiatry,

existentialism, humanism and mental sickness and suicide. Mental sickness is a by-product of a sick logic that meditates on the wrong things rather than on YaH's Word, Truth and Promise. It regards the Word of God as a "relation of events" rather than *truth*. A sick logic can also affect the biochemistry of the body, but the trigger point is sick logic.

> *Let no man deceive himself. If any man among you thinks that he is wise in this age, he must become foolish, so that he may become wise.*

> 1 Corinthians 3:18

Sick minds created psychology, through the lies of existentialism and humanism, and psychology has created the monster of a sick humanity. It is a vicious cycle and who can help us get out of it? According to existentialism we cannot get out of it, which is why most psychiatrists say these all too familiar words to their patients, "This is your sickness, this is your reality, so you must take meds to cope with it for the rest of your life." and "You are mentally sick, schizophrenic (insert label of the day) and there is no way out, only drugs and psychoanalysis can help you cope with it."

But the Word of Yah (God) tells us we can get out of this trap through Messiah Yeshua!

> *Wretched man that I am! Who will set me free from the body of this death? Thanks be to God through Yeshua the Messiah our Lord!*

> 1 Corinthians 7:24,25

He was crushed for our iniquities; the chastening for our well-being (shalom) fell upon Him, and by His scourging we are healed.

Isaiah 53:5

The key is to put Him and His Word at the *center* of your meditation and *speech* instead of *yourself* and your feelings and twisted sense of reality!

A Money Making Machine

Psychology+ Psychiatry+ Pharmaceuticals = $$$$

The child of Existentialism, namely Psychology, has created a financial giant of an industry. It has become a source of income for many sick people who play roles as "doctors" of humanity that give validity to the sickness of mankind instead of calling it to *repentance*. Sick human beings are their "patients", but the Truth is that both "doctor" and "patient" are sick with *sin* and its by-product: *the curse.*

"The wages of sin is death, but the gift of God is eternal life in Yeshua HaMashiach our Lord."

Romans 6:23

The only way out is by changing our idolatrous, self-centered, existential "logic" into the Logos, the Word of Truth written in the Bible and manifested in the flesh (in human form) as Yeshua the Jewish Messiah. When we put our full trust in Him, the Living Word, and in His written Word of instruction and promise (the Bible, the Logos), then our logic gets healed. As a result our mind gets healed from the ravages of sin and death and from the false treatment of Existential-humanism through psychology and psychiatry.

And the Word became flesh, and dwelt among us, and we saw His glory, glory as of the only begotten from the Father, full of grace and truth.

John 1:14

Once the Word of YHVH becomes *flesh* in our mind and mouth, then we are *free* from the slavery of self-centered feelings and circumstances. Then we are *free* from psychological problems! YHVH created everything by His Word and He is well able to recreate our minds, neurotransmitters and brain biochemistry with His Word as we meditate on it and declare it! The Word of Yah (God) in our minds and on our lips is the best medication in the universe!

My son, give attention to my words; incline your ear to my sayings. Do not let them depart from your sight; keep them in the midst of your heart. For they are life to those who find them and health to all their body.

Proverbs 4:20-22

He sent His word and healed them, and delivered them from their destructions.

Psalm 107:20

You shall know the truth and the truth shall make you free.

John 8:32

Existentialism Is a Type of Satanic Worship

Psychology and Psychiatry have sought to dethrone the Creator and enthrone the author of deadly existentialism – Satan, previously named Lucifer.

> *You said in your heart: "I will ascend to the heavens; I will raise my throne above the stars of God; I will sit enthroned on the mount of assembly, on the utmost heights of Mount Zaphon. I will ascend above the tops of the clouds. I will make myself like the Most High.", but you are brought down to the realm of the dead, to the depths of the pit.*

Isaiah 14:13-15

Psychology and psychiatry, that has *man* at the Center (*I will*) rather than Elohim and His Word, is a Satanic religion par excellence! The governments of the Western world are funding Satanism through psychology and psychiatry, preparing an entire generation for the Mark of the Beast and the Anti-Christ, Anti Messiah!

Since man is in the Center and man is allowed to do anything that "feels good" to alleviate his suffering, then, when the option is between the Mark of the Beast or trusting in God, droves of people are ready to alleviate their suffering through the Mark of the Beast. Psychology and its derivative, Psychiatry, have prepared a whole generation to go to hell. (Revelation 13:17; 14:9-11)

The Antidote To The Deadly Sick Logic

The Apostle Paul defeated the lie of philosophy and existentialism, which comes from Greek Philosophy, through the demonstration of Kingdom Power:

And my message and my preaching were not in persuasive words of wisdom (philosophy), but in demonstration of the Spirit and of power.

1 Cor. 2:4

Only the public demonstration of Elohim's Power can fully demolish the stronghold of lies in Existentialism and, therefore, Humanism, in this present day and hour. Experiencing the Power of Elohim, through preaching coupled with signs, wonders and miracles, demolishes the philosophy of Existentialism. It dethrones the lie of humanism that "man created God", and the lie propagated by Existential Religion that says, "God was created for man." Within both of these lies, man is at the center.

In Existentialism, interpreting the world through your reality as a human being becomes the central subject replacing the Creator and His Word. When people experience the Power of Elohim, then His Power becomes their reality. This new and accurate reality disqualifies the lie of Existentialism, that states that man is at the Center and this reality cannot be transcended by "something greater" (God's Power). Elohim's Power has been given to the believers in Yeshua,

"All power has been given unto Me, therefore you GO..."

Matthew 28:18,19

And He called the twelve together, and gave them power and authority over all the demons and to heal diseases. And He sent them out to proclaim the kingdom of God and to perform healing.

Luke 9:1-2

We are equipped with Elohim's Truth and Power to defeat Existentialism and free man from Satan's grip which is leading him to hell. However, the Gospel is not a religion that condemns suffering humanity, but instead, it offers compassion from the Creator who sent His Son to die in our place. Therefore, all of Yeshua's miracles were moved by *compassion*.

"For God so loved the world, that He gave His only begotten Son, that whoever believes in Him shall not perish, but have eternal life.

John 3:16

Experiencing the Power of Elohim coupled with retraining the mind to use healthy logic, based on Yah's (God's) Word, is the basis for healing all sick minds and hearts. In some cases, people must be retrained their minds while still taking medication because they are already caught up in the Psychiatric System. Nevertheless, the Word of God will do its work and heal the mind! In many cases the Creator will eventually open the way to be free from drugs altogether. That is called *a miracle*! When those miracles happen (and they will happen more and more), they are undeniable. Additionally, many other miracles also happen during the process of retraining.

CHAPTER FIVE

The Power of the Word

As stated in the previous chapter, experiencing the Power of Elohim coupled with retraining the mind to use healthy *logic*, based on Yah's (God's) Word, is the basis for healing all sick minds and hearts. Within this context, we must acknowledge two of the most powerful tools available to us:

First, meditating, and second, declaring and obeying the Biblical Logos (Word of God or Bible). This results in the healing of memories and allows us to access our Holy Spirit guided imagination.

> *And do not be conformed to this world, but be transformed by the renewing of your mind, so that you may prove what the will of God is, that which is good and acceptable and perfect.*
>
> Romans 12:2

True Stability

Forever, O YHVH, Your word is settled in heaven.

Psalm 119:89

True stability and emotional wellbeing does not depend on circumstances. The only immutable, stable factor in the world is the Word of the Creator. In the Garden of Eden, where everything was absolutely perfect, the world of Adam was destabilized by rejecting the Commandment of the Creator.

Adam, in male and female form, had no problems at all. In Eden their neurotransmitters worked just fine; they had no childhood traumas or anything that would cause mental instability. However, we eventually find them both hiding behind the trees of the Garden with obvious "paranoia", fear and shame. Any psychiatrist would have diagnosed them, at that point, as traumatized and mentally unstable with an impaired sense of judgment and perception!

They saw their world from a twisted point of view since, to the naked eye, nothing had really changed in the Garden of Eden. The fruit trees, the beautiful animals, and rivers filled with gold were all there as before. However, they were obviously suffering from terrible anxiety and panic attacks! What happened to the Father and Mother of all human beings? What kind of psychotherapy could restore them back to their former healthy and happy state? What drug could have been given to them to put their troubled mind at rest?

Of course this sounds preposterous, anyone who has read the Holy Book knows the cause for the mental change of that

First Couple. There was a 'before and after' situation! Before they listened to the snake and after they listened to the wrong logos.

Before they listened to the tempting words of the snake, their minds were *one* with the Creator of life and their logic was healthy, well-adjusted and happy. After they listened to the sick-logic of the snake (causing them to disbelieve Elohim and His Commandment and to *doubt* His perfect love toward them), they became *sick* in their logic! For the first time in their existence, they had doubt, unbelief and lust for what Elohim had forbidden (the Tree of Knowledge of Good and Evil). After eating of the Tree of Death, they were infected with a terrible mental sickness: their emotions were impaired as fear and dread became part of their mental make-up. Shame invaded their being causing a terrible inferiority complex! One moment before the snake's logos penetrated their being they were totally whole, and one moment later, they were totally sick in their minds!

What You Believe Determines Your Mental Health!

Now faith is the assurance of things hoped for, the conviction of things not seen.

Hebrews 11:1

Contrary to what psychology concentrates on (which is primarily our feelings), our mental health is determined by faith, not feelings. Faith is a spiritual force so great, that it can change a mind from sick to healthy and it is more potent, powerful and effective than any drug and any treatment. Faith does not depend on circumstances or feelings and it stands independently of these things. Faith only needs one thing -- something or someone to lean on. If the object that *faith* leans on is stable, unmovable and immutable, then FAITH can heal an individual's mind and turn it from sick to whole. Let us inspect a few popular objects of faith and see if they pass the test of stability.

Faith In Money

For the love of money is a root of all sorts of evil, and some by longing for it have wandered away from the faith and pierced themselves with many griefs.

1 Timothy 6:10

Many people put their faith in money. If they have plenty of it they feel stable and happy, but when it disappears, they become completely unstable. Financial problems are the number one cause for family strife and divorce.

Do not weary yourself to gain wealth, cease from your consideration of it. When you set your eyes on it, it is gone. For wealth certainly makes itself wings like an eagle that flies toward the heavens.

Proverbs 23:4-5

Can faith in money cause permanent stability and health in our minds and emotions? The answer is a resolute *no* and as the saying goes: "Money comes, and money goes" and so will our mental health if it depends on money!

YHVH is my shepherd, I shall not want.

Psalm 23:1

Faith In Myself

Yet you do not know what your life will be like tomorrow. You are just a vapor that appears for a little while and then vanishes away.

Yaakov (James) 4:14

It is very popular today to have faith in oneself as if the human being is all-powerful. This god of self is very easy to dethrone. Human beings are very unstable and untrustworthy; we change according to circumstances and even the strongest one among us can break down and collapse at any moment. If you base your stability on yourself and your abilities to cope with everything, you are setting yourself up for a *big fall*! No human being has ever been infallible, not even the first human in the Garden of Eden. Even the best of us falter and disappointed ourselves and others.

A healthy sense of self-worth is very important, but we cannot base our life of *faith* on ourselves, as we are not stable, unchanging or immutable. Strong winds and storms can uproot and break the strongest of 'trees.' When that happens, we must find the One who is greater than ourselves!

A voice says, "Call out. "Then he answered, "What shall I call out? "All flesh is grass, and all its loveliness is like the flower of the field. The grass withers, the flower fades, when the breath of the Lord blows upon it; surely the people are grass. The grass withers, the flower fades, but the word of our God stands forever.

Isaiah 40:6-8

Faith In Religion

They said, "Come, let us build for ourselves a city, and a tower whose top will reach into heaven, and let us make for ourselves a name, otherwise we will be scattered abroad over the face of the whole earth.

Genesis 11:4

First of all let us define Religion as "man's attempt to create a god of his own liking." Every religious system is based on man's perception of who God is and how to reach Him.

They said to one another, "Come, let us make bricks and burn them thoroughly." And they used brick for stone, and they used tar for mortar.

Genesis 11:3

The problem with religion is that it is man-made, and like everything else that man makes, it is perishable and unstable. There is no building or system that humans have built, that cannot be brought down and overthrown. Just remember 9/11 and the mighty Twin Towers in New York City. In the same way every religious system can collapse and become unstable. Faith in one religion or another, with all its traditions and liturgies, can cause a false sense of stability and identity for a while, but it does not have the real power to heal the sick mind or to stabilize neurotransmitters. It is definitely the best placebo invented by man, but a placebo is not a cure. Religion is not based on *truth*, which is immutable, but on human perception of God and the World. We have already mentioned how human perception can be impaired when listening to the wrong logos, to the wrong source. Just like Adam in the Garden had an impaired perception of his circumstances and of the Creator, so every religious system has a *different* perception of "god", the "cosmic force" or the "supreme being." That of course lends itself to two evils: the first is Dogmatism – "My god is the only true God" or "My religion is the only true Religion", which can lead to hatred, racial discrimination and even murder in the name of "god." Second is Confusion – If everyone believes in a different "god" which one is the real One? And if one "god" disappoints me, as it does not deliver the "goods" that I need, such as mental stability and happiness, can we change "gods" at any given time? That is very disorienting and certainly unstable!

> *All of us like sheep have gone astray, each of us has turned to his own way;, but YHVH has caused the iniquity of us all to fall on Him (Yeshua).*

> Isaiah 53:1

Faith In the Universe

For they exchanged the truth of God for a lie, and worshiped and served the creature rather than the Creator, who is blessed forever. Amen.

Romans 1:25

Positive thinking and faith in the Universe is one of the most popular religions of the 21st Century. Many are flocking to it through various trainings and techniques. It is very interesting that this religion is actually, for the most part, based on the Logos, Word or Logic, found in the Books of the Bible. It uses principles that are written there, such as the importance of positive confession, sowing and reaping, giving and the like.

This particular *faith* is the most exciting and stable of all, but it has one flaw: it is still very unstable as all of the universal elements are very unstable.

Lately we have been experiencing Global Warming and, even with all our faith in the Universe, we are not able to change that predicament. In reality, the Universe is very unstable and far from being in harmony. Our faith in the Universe cannot save us from bankruptcy, or from loss of life due to weather instability. The mere fact that the Universe cannot be fully trusted can cause terrible anxiety. What if the Universe turns against me, what then? What can the five hundred thousand victims of the terrible Tsunami in Thailand say about the goodness of the Universe? Most of them were firm believers in the elements, they talked to the winds, to the stones and to all of creation, but it still did not help them when the Tsunami came. Trees can be uprooted, and rocks can disintegrate – this is not a source of stability!

The voice of YHVH is powerful, the voice of YHVH is majestic. The voice of YHVH breaks the cedars; Yes, YHVH breaks in pieces the cedars of Lebanon.

Psalm 29:4,5

The Only Proven Stable Object of Faith In the World

We established the fact that *faith* has the power to heal a sick mind, but *faith* cannot stand alone – it needs an object to lean on. All of the above objects, regardless of how popular they are, have proven unstable at one time or another. We cannot expect lasting stability and mind wholeness if our faith leans on an unstable object (money, self, religion or the universe). Faith that leans on any of these is bound to eventually bring disappointment. When that disappointment sets in, it can cause a true mental breakdown, confusion, and instability beyond imagination!

There is only one thing that has never changed and has proven true throughout all generations: The Logos, the Word of Elohim The Creator! By His Word He established the heavens and the earth, and they still exists. He created Adam-Man, and we still exist. His laws are absolute Truth, and if violated, cause instability.

The Word of Elohim establishes that the Earth is a round planet and early Christian scholars, like Hermannus Contractus (1013-1054) and Thomas Aquinas (1225-1274) saw the Biblical texts and the scientific evidence as being congruent concepts. This was later firmly established as irrefutable Truth when Christopher Columbus sailed to the New World and Ferdinand Magellan circumnavigated the Earth (1519-21).

It is He who sits above the circle of the earth, and its inhabitants are like grasshoppers, who stretches out the heavens like a curtain And spreads them out like a tent to dwell in.

Isaiah 40:22

The Law of Gravity is always there -- if you defy it you can be crushed.

He established the earth upon its foundations, so that it will not totter forever and ever.

Psalm 104:5

He established night and day and all the seasons.

Yours is the day, Yours also is the night; You have prepared the light and the sun. You have established all the boundaries of the earth; You have made summer and winter.

Psalm 74:16,17

The Law of sowing and reaping always works. Whatever you sow, you reap.

While the earth remains, seedtime and harvest, and cold and heat, And summer and winter, And day and night Shall not cease.

Genesis 8:22

The Law of Rest (Shabbat), if violated, causes people to break down.

Then God blessed the seventh day and sanctified it, because in it He rested from all His work which God had created and made.

Genesis 2:3, Deuteronomy 5:12

The Law of the Curse that reoccurs throughout three or four generations is proven by the Medical Science as Genetic Family Problems. That is why mental sickness, cancer, heart disease and the like "run in families."

You shall not make for yourself an idol, or any likeness of what is in heaven above or on the earth beneath or in the water under the earth. You shall not worship them or serve them; for I, the Lord your God, am a jealous God, visiting the iniquity of the fathers on the children, and on the third and the fourth generations of those who hate Me, but showing lovingkindness to thousands, to those who love Me and keep My commandments.

Deuteronomy 5:8-10

He chose Israel as His People, the Land of Israel as their land and Jerusalem as their Capital. In spite of all exiles and persecutions, the People of Israel still exist, and so does the Land of Israel and the City of Jerusalem. You can have different "political opinions", but Truth is Truth and Reality is Reality. YHVH spoke it in His Word and it has come to pass in front of our very eyes!

But Judah will be inhabited forever and Jerusalem for all generations. And I will avenge their blood which I have not avenged, for YHVH dwells in Zion.

Joel 3:20,21

YHVH will possess Judah as His portion in the holy land, and will again choose Jerusalem. "Be silent, all flesh, before the Lord; for He is aroused from His holy habitation."

Zechariah 2:12,13

These are only a few of the many witnesses that Elohim's Word is stable, immovable and totally *true*. When we put all our trust in what He says, in His Logos, we will never collapse! Faith in Him and His Word is sure ground and our foundation for mental health.

From the end of the earth will I cry unto thee, when my heart is overwhelmed: lead me to the rock that is higher than I.

Psalm 61:2 KJV

CHAPTER SIX

The Great Transformation

Once we have chosen to put our trust in the Creator and His Word, a huge transformation happens to our mind. The more we meditate, speak and obey His Word, the healthier we become! It starts by letting go of our old lifestyle of doubt, unbelief, fear, shame and rebellion. We now reject the logos of the snake and choose the Logos of the Creator!

I beseech you therefore, brethren, by the mercies of God, that you present your bodies a living sacrifice, holy, acceptable to God, which is your reasonable service. And do not be conformed to this world, but be transformed by the renewing of your mind, that you may prove what is that good and acceptable and perfect will of God.

Romans 12:1-2

The Logos of the Creator recreates in us with a healthy logic. Our minds have been renewed and we reject the sick-logic based on the lies of the snake. Now we believe in Elohim's love for us, we do not doubt His motives, and we can trust His ways.

For My thoughts are not your thoughts, nor are your ways My ways," says YHVH. "For as the heavens are higher than the earth, so are My ways higher than your ways, and My thoughts than your thoughts.

Isaiah 55:8,9

The Plumb-Line of Trust!

Trusting in YHVH with all your heart and lean not unto your own understanding.

Proverbs 3:5

The key for mental health is a faith that leans completely on YHVH's Word, His Nature, Ability and Willingness to do us good. That kind of faith develops a deep *trust* in Adonai (Lord). That deep trust makes us mentally and emotionally stable, able to overcome every adverse circumstance. How do we develop such *trust* and what does *trust* really mean?

In Hebrew the word for *trust* is *bitcha*. Bitcha comes from the root word for security, which implies absolute protection. In order to have such security in His absolute love and protection, we have to let go of our own self-protection. We are living in a fallen world with great and many dangers. Life itself has taught us to be very guarded and self-protective in order to avoid unnecessary pain and suffering. That is, of course, quite logical; however, that is leaning into our own understanding of security. We believe that security comes from living in fortified houses, from insurance agents, from medical insurance and savings accounts. While all these are good, there is absolutely no certainty that any of these things can protect us from pain, suffering or calamities. The ability of YHVH to protect us from this dark world goes far beyond what we can normally do to protect ourselves.

Behold, He who keeps Israel shall neither slumber nor sleep.

Psalm 121:4

In Psalm 121 it says that He never slumbers or sleeps as He watches over Israel, and this applies to both the People of Israel and to those that have joined the Commonwealth of Israel through the Blood of Yeshua's sacrifice. True faith will lead us to a place of rest. While we may be sleeping or resting, He does not slumber or sleep! However, to come to a place of such confidence in His Love and Protection, we must work it through. There is something that we need to do, and that something is called *prayer*. It is not just any kind of 'religious' prayer, but rather *effective prayer*.

Most of the mental problems come from a place of deep anxiety and fears, and the only cure for this is *bitcha*, deep trust in Elohim's Word, His Nature, Willingness and Ability to protect us even in the midst of hell!

If I ascend into heaven, You are there; If I make my bed in hell, behold, You are there.

Psalm 139:8

But how do we work this through?

Be anxious for nothing, *but in everything by prayer and supplication, with* thanksgiving, *let your requests be made known to God; and the peace of God, which surpasses all understanding, will guard your hearts and minds through Messiah Yeshua.*

Philippians 4:6,7

Be anxious for *nothing* is actually a commandment, however it is easier said than done! As I mentioned earlier, most mental and emotional problems are triggered by deep-seated fears and anxieties. That is why Elohim speaks to us through the Apostle Paul who clearly tells us the remedy for mental health is to "Be anxious for nothing..."

Then He goes on to instruct us regarding how to obtain this blissful condition: "by prayer, supplication, with thanksgiving..." in our hearts we will obtain a shalom, a wellbeing that is beyond our understanding.

The only way to have this shalom, this wellbeing that surpasses our understanding, knowledge, and experience, is by not leaning unto our own understanding and taking the following steps to obtain bitcha (deep confidence and trust that makes us completely stable):

Petitions: Faith In His Word

Ask and it shall be given unto you. This is the Prayer of Faith, and it is always based on the Word of Yah and His Promises.

You have to petition Him based on His Word in order to obtain a favorable answer.

If you abide in Me, and My words abide in you, you will ask what you desire, and it shall be done for you.

John 15:7

There are two conditions for prayer to be favorably answered. We need to abide in Him, which means that we have surrendered our lives to Him and have turned our back on the world and sin. As long as we still lust for the world and all that is in it, we will not obtain answered prayer. A good prayer would be "YHVH, make me to love what you love and to hate what you hate."

We need to have His Word abide in us. In other words we need to read the Word, meditate on it, speak it and sing it until it becomes part of us, so when we pray we believe His Word. Faith comes by hearing and hearing the Word of Yah. Without faith in His Word we can't please Him, and our prayers will not be favorably answered. (Hebrews 11:6)

I remember one time I was praying and Yeshua spoke to me very sternly, "Dominiquae! I am a lawyer! If you want to obtain anything from me, state your case!" In other words, "Ask me according to My Word." He was saying, "I cannot answer your 'emotional prayers' without them being backed up by *My* Word."

Most people get frustrated with Yah because he does not answer them, but without going through the above-mentioned motions, He has no commitment to answer us.

Supplication: Faith In His Nature

Only when we believe that He is totally Good, Just, Merciful and True, can really supplicate before Him. He loves to do us good and to assist us, but He can only do it if we are in faith. This faith believes that *He is* and that He is a *rewarder* of those who diligently seek Him (Hebrews 11:6). We can know His will and obey it. He loves to give us good things to enjoy; He loves to reward us and surprise us with wonderful things. His Holy Nature is to be totally *good*!

Just look at the beauty of nature, the flowers, the corals, the fish, the babies. He is just so beautiful and good, but you must believe that He is Good, and willing to do good, in order to supplicate before Him in the right way.

If you then, being evil, know how to give good gifts to your children, how much more will your Father who is in heaven give good things to those who ask Him!

Matthew 7:11

Look at Hannah, the barren wife of Elkana, who could have no babies: her desperate supplication was answered beyond her understanding! She bore Samuel, whom she dedicated to the service of Adonai, and he became the Prophet of Israel who anointed Kings Saul and David. And afterwards Yah gave Hannah five more children, though she only asked Him for one. That is how good He is: always doing much more than we can imagine. (1 Samuel 1-2)

And the YHVH visited Hannah, so that she conceived and bore three sons and two daughters. Meanwhile the child Samuel grew before YHVH.

1 Samuel 2:2

Thanksgiving: Faith In His Ability to Act

We must trust Yah's power and ability to do what He has said in His Word. We must trust that He has the power to grant our correctly requested petitions. We must trust that Elohim can do the impossible! This definitely requires us to not lean on our own limited understanding and try to figure out how He will do what we have asked of Him. We do not know the 'how' or the 'when', so instead of 'figuring it out' (which is an act of unbelief and pride), we simply *thank* and praise Him *before* any manifestation happens. The act of *thanksgiving* releases Yah's ability, including His Angelic Host to work on our behalf!

But I am afflicted and in pain; May Your salvation, O God, set me securely on high. I will praise the name of God with song And magnify Him with thanksgiving. And it will please the Lord better than an ox Or a young bull with horns and hoofs.

Psalm 69:29-31

Bless YHVH, you His angels, who excel in strength, who do His word, Heeding the voice of His word. Bless YHVH, all you His hosts, You ministers of His, who do His pleasure.

Bless YHVH, all His works, In all places of His dominion.
Bless YHVH, O my soul.

Psalm 103:20-22

The outcome of obedience to the Commandment "Be anxious for nothing..." will be *shalom* beyond all comprehension and wellbeing beyond your imagination. You will experience extravagant answers to your prayers and petitions, but in His way and His *timing*! This shalom is the deep trust, the *bitcha*, that causes us to be stable, immovable and whole in our minds. This kind of trust never loses heart and sails through all seasons of life in *shalom*.

Review

Petition Yah with prayers of faith in His Word. Supplicate Him from the depth of your heart with faith in His Nature to do you good. Thank Him before any manifestation happens, showing faith in His ability to answer you beyond your imagination.

Continue singing and praising with total trust in His goodness and ability to protect you and to bless you. Even if it takes 40 years, like it took for Joshua and Caleb to enter the Promised Land, His answer will not delay. Whether one minute, one year or two thousand years, as long as you practice "be anxious for nothing" and take all the above-mentioned steps, you will be *well*!

CHAPTER SEVEN

What Are You Leaning On?

*Trust in YHVH with all your heart and do not lean on
your own understanding. In all your ways acknowledge
Him, and He will make your paths straight.*

Proverbs 3:5,6

In the previous chapters we have established the fact that, in order to be healthy mentally and emotionally, we need to have faith that leans on a stable and immovable object. We have reached the conclusion that the only Object of our faith that is completely stable and immovable is the Word of YHVH, the Creator of the Universe! We have understood that complete trust (bitcha) in His Word, His Nature, and Ability, is the key for stability. To lean on our own understanding, our own thoughts, emotions, opinions or interpretations of circumstances is a recipe for disaster. Our mind is too frail and so is our nervous system. Even the strongest of us can break down under some circumstances.

Supermen & Women Can Break!

For He Himself knows our frame; He is mindful that we are but dust.

Psalm 103:14

Let me give you a personal example. I was regarded as a "super woman" prior to my salvation experience. I was married to a precious man, but he was bi-polar (Manic-Depressive disorder). His mental sickness manifested right after the birth of my second child, my son Yuval. He went into a terrible depression, and every night he would lay awake telling me that I was going to collapse and go into bankruptcy. At that time, I was a very promising health food store owner and Health Consultant. I owned two successful stores and a clinic. My health columns appeared weekly in a local magazine in the Sharon area of Israel. I was a champion and pioneer of in-home natural birth and became very famous after the birth of my son Yuval.

Yuval was born at home even though I had given birth to my daughter Adi via Caesarian section. I was very upset with the doctors who did not have the patience to wait for me to give birth in my own time. They decided to use the knife instead of patience and faith in Elohim's natural process of child birth. In the hospital in Israel, where I birthed Adi, 50% of the women were given over to the knife in the performance of Caesarian sections.

I refused to agree that this is the way things should be. I started my own campaign espousing that the Creator-Elohim had created the woman's body to give birth without any need of medications or knives, except in extreme cases. Even though my obstetrician refused to accompany me in this venture, YHVH, whom I did not personally know at the time, sent me a great midwife and another doctor in case there was any need. Yuval came out to the light of this world proving that the Creator was real, HalleluYah!

Nevertheless, right after his Brit Mila (Covenant of Circumcision), his father fell into a terrible depression, and in his distress dragged us all into the pits of hell. For a year he managed to bring us all to the edge of despair. He refused help or treatment. Though I did not trust conventional psychiatric treatments, I felt I had no other choice. I took him to a psychiatrist who prescribed Lithium, (which is commonly used in cases of a bi-polar condition) which he never took consistently.

I also remember asking the doctor about myself, since I was in terrible anguish and anxiety trying to heal my husband. I was exposed to his constant barrage of negativity and experienced numerous sleepless nights. I was breast feeding my new baby while caring for my 3 yr. old daughter. Additionally, I was handling both stores and the clinic while supplementing our income by working as a tour guide on weekends! I had *no* rest and I had just given birth!

I will never forget what the Psychiatrist told me, "You, with your (strong) character, only need some refreshing time at the swimming pool or the beach and you will be fine." Less than a month later I had complete breakdown. This breakdown effected my whole family, business, clinic and reputation. No one imagined that this strong woman would ever break down!

Beloved readers, there is not one individual who is immune to breaking down given the circumstances. Some break down earlier than others. I was leaning on *myself* and on *my* own understanding as I tried to rescue my husband.

I was looking for Elohim (mostly in the wrong places) but did not know Him. I did pray and eventually Yeshua revealed Himself to me at the waters of the Sea of Galilee in a dramatic way! My book YES! tells you the story of both my breakdown and miraculous salvation.

The father of my children killed himself when they were aged 6 (son Yuval) and 10 (daughter Adi). He refused to put his trust in Yeshua and continued leaning on his emotions, his own thoughts and opinions. His last words to me were, "I will never repent." My last words to him were, "Please do not be arrogant against Elohim!" I am here to tell you that the only difference between a healthy mind and a sick mind is FAITH, but not just any kind of faith. Only faith that leans *completely* on the Word, Nature and Ability of the Creator can bring about a healthy mind!

The steadfast of mind You will keep in perfect wellbeing, because he trusts in You.

Isaiah 26:3

The legacy that the father of my children left to them was so terrible that I have spent years in prayer and action in order to counteract it in their lives. Both of them have challenged me tremendously, and I have walked through mental hospitals many times over many years proclaiming the Word, singing in the Spirit and prophesying Yah's Master Plan over their lives. Due to Yah's faithfulness in answering my heart's steadfast and obedient plea, they are still alive today. They are both in the process of recovering from the ravages of sin, pride, rebellion and the terrible curse of their father's legacy. The battle for their lives has been so fierce that, had I not leaned completely on Yah's Word, His Nature and Ability, I would not have been able to help them and I, also, would have lost my mind, but as I have applied the principles that I write about here, I have stayed stable and whole. This has enabled me to bring many people into stability and wholeness by the authority vested in me to minister in Yah's Word and Power.

I prayed many years ago for YHVH to give me a Gift of Miracles for the mentally sick. Indeed we have seen many people come out of clinical depression (even after 50 years of suffering!), many other afflictions. However, if the miracle is not followed by the transformation of the mind, the fleshly mind can break down again. The *battle is in the mind!* The only way to be whole mentally is to exchange our fleshly mind with the *mind of Messiah!*

For who has known the mind of the Lord, that he will instruct Him? But we have the mind of Messiah.

1 Corinthians 2:16

Mind of Messiah

The steadfast of mind You will keep in perfect wellbeing, because he trusts in You.

Isaiah 26:3

In order to acquire the Mind of Messiah, we need to take the following steps:

- Repent and accept salvation through Yeshua's Blood Sacrifice. Ask and receive forgiveness of all our sins in His name. (John 3:16, Isaiah 61)
- Give Him our life and make Him the owner of our life – spirit, soul and body. (Matthew 7:21-23)
- Get baptized in water by full immersion. This is the first step of obedience. (Mark 16:16)
- Ask and receive the Baptism in the Holy Spirit, with the evidence of speaking in New Tongues. (Acts 2)
- Become a disciple by studying the Bible in its entirety, in its original context, with no Replacement Theology (Appendix A)
- Understand the Holy Scriptures from its Hebrew perspective. (Our GRM Bible School is an excellent place to start – see www.kad-esh.org, then select Bible School).
- Meditate on YHVH, His Word, His Nature and His Plan all day long. (Joshua 1:8, Philippians 4:8)
- Obey His written Commandments and personal Commandments given to you by the Holy Spirit. (Matthew 5:17-20, John 15:10, 14)

- Pray in the Spirit (in tongues) (Jude 20, Romans 8:26-28)

- Pray the Word and declare it day and night until your mouth utters only His Logos (written Word) and Rhema (inspired and prophetic Word) at all times and in all circumstances. The Bible contains promises for the Covenant believer and disciple in every circumstance! Find them and make for yourself Word Prayers. (Proverbs 18:21, Isaiah 55:10,11)

- Pray and ask the Ruach HaKodesh (Holy Spirit) to lead you to the congregation of His choosing. If you were born again under the leadership of some congregation, that is your spiritual family. Unless Yah Himself moves you and you ask for the blessing of your leadership, stay there and serve there. Yah is a God of order, faithfulness and commitment. (Psalm 133)

- Walk in Humility. Submit to your pastors and leaders. Honor authority and follow them as they follow Yeshua. Refrain from criticizing Yah ordained and appointed leadership. No one is perfect. (Hebrews 13:17)

- Forgive all who have hurt you instantly and continually. Do it by faith and not by feelings. Do not allow for a Root of Bitterness to be in your heart. No one deserves forgiveness, but we give it because we have received it. (Matthew 6:14,15, Hebrews 12:14-17)

- Exercise spiritual authority against the devil and all powers of darkness. Walk as a warrior! (Matthew 18:18, Luke 10:19, Ephesians 6:10)

- Be generous and bless others. (Matthew 7:12, 2 Corinthians 9:6-8)

Follow me in the next chapters as we learn how to acquire the Mind of Messiah.

For My thoughts are not your thoughts, nor are your ways My ways," declares YHVH. "For as the heavens are higher than the earth, so are My ways higher than your ways and My thoughts than your thoughts.

Isaiah 55:8-9

CHAPTER EIGHT

The Baptism In the Holy Spirit

The only way to be whole mentally is to exchange our fleshly mind for the *mind of Messiah! "For who has known the mind of the Lord, that he will instruct Him? But we have the mind of Messiah."* (1 Corinthians 2:16) We shall start with the #1 *key* to obtain the Mind of Messiah or the Anointed Mind -- the infilling or Baptism in the Holy Spirit.

The Baptism In the Holy Spirit

But you will receive power when the Holy Spirit has come upon you; and you shall be My witnesses both in Jerusalem, and in all Judea and Samaria, and even to the remotest part of the earth.

Acts 1:8

We cannot attempt to have a completely whole and sound mind without being filled with Yah's Power. His Power is freely given to us when we have submitted our lives to Yeshua, and we ask to be filled by His Ruach (Spirit) – just like the Jewish disciples were as recorded in Acts chapter 2.

And they were all filled with the Holy Spirit and began to speak with other tongues, as the Spirit was giving them utterance.

Acts 2:4

In most cases, after the supernatural occurrence of Acts 2, people received the baptism of the Holy Spirit by the laying on of hands. That was my case!

Being a Jew, and not knowing anything about Christianity, I never heard of the baptism in the Holy Spirit. However, right after my dramatic salvation, a young believer asked me, "Have you received the baptism in the Holy Spirit with speaking in tongues since you have believed?"

That is the exact question that Shimon-Peter asked some disciples about 2000 years ago before he proceeded to lay hands on them!! (Acts 8:15-17)

Then they began laying their hands on them, and they were receiving the Holy Spirit.

Acts 8:17

Having delved into the occult for four and a half months, searching for Elohim in the wrong places, I immediately replied, "Yeshua - *yes*, but *no* spirits, thank you!" This young believer laughed at my fear of spirits and proceeded to lay hands on me as he prayed, "O Father in Heaven, baptize Dominiquae in your Holy Spirit."

As this young man prayed, I immediately felt like I was wrapped in warm blanket of love. I heard the Voice of Messiah telling me, "Go home and burn the Ouija board drawing that you have made, and you will receive." I jumped to my feet immediately, bid the young believer goodbye in haste as I quickly said, "I know how to receive now. I am going home." I caught the bus and arrived at my tiny apartment in Jerusalem where I proceeded to obey the Ruach's (Spirit's) instructions. I watched that Ouija board drawing *burn*. I knew that this had destroyed my life! By seeking for answers from the Almighty through this spirit board, I only encountered demons. As it burned completely, I washed all the ashes down the sink with plenty of water.

A Shower From Heaven!

All of a sudden I was knocked down on my knees as something like a pressure shower opened above my head and began to wash me like a car in the car wash! As this was happening, I started to pray in tongues, languages that I had never known before. From midnight until 5 o'clock in the morning I heard the Voice of Messiah telling me, "I love you; I love you; I love you!" I wept and wept and wept as this shower from Heaven was washing me clean and empowering me to walk a supernatural walk of holiness and wholeness in the midst of a very dark world system.

When I rose to my feet, after 5 hours on my knees on a concrete floor, I had no pain in my knees and I was as light as a feather. The only thing I wanted to do was to sing and praise and praise and sing! I had changed *inside* though *outside* all my circumstances were still the same. And those circumstances were tragic and distressing: I had gone through a terrible divorce, I had lost my children, my stores, my clinic, my friends, my hair was falling out in chunks and my reputation was "down the tubes." I was penniless, living in a dump, and even worms were coming out of my shower drain! I was heart-broken and destitute, having lost everything. After accepting Yeshua and being filled with the Ruach HaKodesh (Holy Spirit) I had gained *everything*!

Beloved do not allow anyone to fool you with the doctrines of demons and men! Without the baptism in the Holy Spirit, with praying in tongues, we cannot walk in any kind of victory. I praise Yah that I did not know any doctrines so He could give me *all* He had for me. Remember *that all* those Jewish believers, who were in the Upper Room of the Temple, got filled with the Holy Spirit praying in different tongues and languages that they had never heard before. That is exactly what happened to me, and no one had ever explained it – I had never even heard of it!, but the *fruit* of it was Heavenly and it still is.

Many people are walking religious, dry, bitter, judgmental and fleshly lives because they have opposed the baptism in the Holy Spirit and, especially, speaking in tongues. Why would they do that? Why would they torpedo their own walk? Because Satan is deathly afraid of empowered believers!

You can never obtain the Mind of Messiah and be completely whole without the empowerment of the Holy Spirit! Neither can you be released into Yah's Service. That is why He told them to wait in Jerusalem and to receive *before* they did anything for

Him and His Kingdom. Shimon-Peter was a coward who denied the Master prior to his execution on Golgotha, but after he was baptized with the Holy Spirit and Fire, he became a fearless, bold witness of Messiah – unafraid of men or death! Under the Power of the Holy Spirit the first 3000 people in Israel were saved at the bold preaching of Peter!

So then, those who had received his word were baptized; and that day there were added about three thousand souls.

Acts 2:41

Through the Book of Jude we receive this instruction: in order to be built up in our faith, we must pray in the Holy Spirit (pray in tongues), and this is the way to stay in the *love* of Yah (God). We have established that *fear* and *anxiety* is a major cause of mental problems – the Holy Scriptures show us that the only antidote against fear and anxiety is faith and love. In order to build ourselves in faith and be filled with the Love of our Abba (Father), we must pray in the Holy Spirit or pray in tongues of Elohim and Angels! These are not known tongues, but unknown tongues, and it is a *sign* that we are filled with His Spirit. There are many other gifts that come with the Baptism in the Holy Spirit, but this is not a *gift*, it is a *sign*. All the other gifts can be stirred up and released when we pray and worship in tongues!

But you, beloved, building yourselves up on your most holy faith, praying in the Holy Spirit, keep yourselves in the love of God, waiting anxiously for the mercy of our Lord Yeshua HaMashiach to eternal life.

Jude 20-21

In the Book of Romans we see that we cannot even pray correctly unless the Holy Spirit prays through us, and He prays through groaning and sounds that are not our normal language!

In the same way the Spirit also helps our weakness; for we do not know how to pray as we should, but the Spirit Himself intercedes for us with groanings too deep for words; and He who searches the hearts knows what the mind of the Spirit is, because He intercedes for the saints according to the will of God.

Romans 8:26-27

As a matter of fact, only when we yield to the Ruach to pray through us will we be praying the right prayers which will bring about His desired results – and will cause all things to work together for good for us!

And we know that God causes all things to work together for good to those who love God, to those who are called according to His purpose.

Romans 8:28

Praying In Tongues

- Builds us up in our most Holy Faith. Jude 20
- Keeps us filled with Elohim's Love. Jude 21

- Keeps us connected to the Power of Yah like electricity flows through a plug causing us to pray correctly according to Yah's will. Romans 8:26-28
- Empowers us to exercise spiritual warfare against Satan and all darkness. Ephesians 6:10-18
- Refills us with the Spirit when we pray and sing in tongues (spiritual songs!). Ephesians 5:17-19
- Helps us to die to our fleshly thoughts and brings about the Mind of Messiah.
- Causes *all* things to work together for good for us! Yes, even Satan has to submit and work together for our good when we pray in tongues or in the Spirit! (*All* things *are all* things! HaleluYAH!)
- Assist us in praying prophetically as we pray for interpretation of our tongues and we flow in the understanding from there.

"What is the conclusion then? I will pray with the spirit, and I will also pray with the understanding. I will sing with the spirit, and I will also sing with the understanding"

1 Corinthians 14:15

Important Disclaimer!

When you prophecy or pray a specific prayer in tongues that you want people to agree to, you must pray for interpretation, but praying in tongues and worshipping in tongues requires no interpretation, as it is not a message for people, but rather a conversation between you and Yah. It can also be part of spiritual warfare, a prayer of battle against the powers of darkness! (Mark 16:17, Ephesians 6:10-18, Romans 8:26-27)

He who speaks in a tongue edifies himself, but he who prophesies edifies the church. I wish you all spoke with tongues, but even more that you prophesied; for he who prophesies is greater than he who speaks with tongues, unless indeed he interprets, that the church may receive edification.

1 Corinthians 14:4, 5

Every time that you decide to prophesy publicly in tongues, pray for interpretation so others may be edified, but if you are praying in tongues together with other believers who are also praying in tongues, or alone without public prophecy, then there is no need for interpretation since you are all glorifying Yah together and, are being built up in the faith in unison, as an act of worship.

In order to have the Mind of Messiah we must be baptized in the Holy Spirit, causing us to pray and sing much in tongues – then move into praying or singing with understanding prophetically in order to edify others. Praying and singing in tongues helps us release prophetic songs and prophetic utterances, which is the Mind of Messiah!

The Spirit of Prophecy is the testimony of Yeshua.

Revelation 19:10b

CHAPTER NINE

Spiritual Warfare

The only way to be whole mentally is to exchange our fleshly mind for the *mind of Messiah*! *"For who has known the mind of the Lord, that he will instruct Him? But we have the mind of Messiah."* 1 Corinthians 2:16

Therefore I urge you, brethren, by the mercies of God, to present your bodies a living and holy sacrifice, acceptable to God, which is your spiritual service of worship. And do not be conformed to this world, but be transformed by the renewing of your mind, so that you may prove what the will of God is, that which is good and acceptable and perfect.

Romans 12:1-2

Put on the full armor of God, so that you will be able to stand firm against the schemes of the devil. For our struggle is not against flesh and blood, but against the rulers, against the powers, against the world forces of this darkness, against the spiritual forces of wickedness in the heavenly places.

Ephesians 6: 11-12

We have already stated that there is a battle, which awaits the believer in Messiah, and the battle is mainly in the mind. If we win the battle of the mind, we will be victorious in all battles!

In order to win the battle of the mind, we have to wear the Mind of Messiah, and this is how to do it:

For the weapons of our warfare are not of the flesh, but divinely powerful for the destruction of fortresses. We are destroying speculations and every lofty thing raised up against the knowledge of God, and we are taking every thought captive to the obedience of Messiah.

2 Corinthians 10:4-5

- Command your mind to be *captive* to Messiah. 2 Corinthians 10:5
- Believe Yah's Word in every situation. Hebrews 11:6
- Meditate and Declare His Word of Promise without ceasing. Isaiah 55:10,11
- Do not trust your feelings and emotions automatically. Philippians 3:3, Jeremiah 17:4-6, 9-10
- Do not trust any circumstances as the true reality of Elohim for you. Everything is subject to change. Hebrews 11:1
- Reject evil reports about your situation. John 8:43-45

- Do not trust your own interpretations of your circumstances unless revealed by the Holy Spirit or by wise council with wise and godly people.
- Forget about your own opinions. Romans 8:7
- Do not worry about the opinions of others unless they match the Scriptures and the promises Yah has given you. 1 Corinthians 2:15, Romans 3:4
- Be humble to receive correction from those who are pastoring you. Hebrews 13:17
- Exercise authority over the devil, all demons and their demonic actions. Luke 10:19, Matthew 18:18, Psalm 149:8-9
- Trust Yah even if the outcome of your prayers is not what you imagined. Proverbs 3:5

Even Yeshua did not know the full plan until He was hanging from the Cross having taken on the sin of the world. In that moment, the Ruach HaKodesh withdrew from Him until all righteousness was fulfilled, but even in Yeshua's pain, when He felt forsaken, He reminded those who could hear His voice of the divine plan of His Father as He cried out the first line of Psalms 22, knowing they could recite the rest from memory, "Abba, Abba why have you forsaken me?"

At the end of it all He rose from the dead and He is now sitting at the Right Hand of the Father bringing many sons and daughters to Glory due to His obedience unto death!

It is mandatory that you will exercise authority over the Powers of Darkness, especially as it pertains to your mind, and to the lives of those under your care, in your sphere of authority and service. Walk in full authority, which is possible only when you are walking under the authority of the Holy Spirit, His Word and your God appointed leaders!

Remember that the battle is always in your mind. What you believe inside will dictate the course of your tongue (speech) and your tongue will dictate the course of your life!

I cannot stress enough the fact that you have to line up your thoughts and speech with Yah's Word of Covenant Promise – then, of course, your Actions will follow. Keep walking obediently by faith in the midst of all circumstances. As you do, hold on to the certainty that *all* things are working *together* for your greater good! (Romans 8:28)

And without faith it is impossible to be well-pleasing unto him; for he that cometh to God must believe that he is, and that he is a rewarder of them that seek after him.

Hebrews 1:6

Weapons of Warfare

- Praying In Tongues: Jude 20, Romans 8:26-28
- Binding and Losing Matthew 18:18
- Declaring the Word: Proverbs 18:21, Job 22:28
- Praising In Music and Dance: Psalm 149-150
- Clapping Hands: Psalm 47:1
- Blowing Shofars: Joshua 6
- Shouting: Joshua 6:1-5
- Giving: 2 Corinthians 9:6-8, Isaiah 32:8
- Forgiveness: Mark 11; 25-26

- Overcome Evil With Good – Blessing Others: Romans 12:21
- Stand Your Ground and Resist the Devil: Yaakov (James) 4:7
- Stay busy in the work that He has given you to do: 2 Timothy 2:15

And the God of peace shall bruise Satan under your feet shortly. The grace of our Lord Yeshua the Messiah be with you.

Romans 16:20

CHAPTER TEN

On Purpose – Davka!

The word davka in colloquial Hebrew means "resolutely on purpose" and it is sometimes used as an insolent word; other times it is used as a word that denotes boldness and perseverance against all odds! It is an aggressive word and it defies passivity.

The wicked flee when no one pursues, but the righteous are bold as a lion.

Proverbs 28:1

It is a diehard kind of word – It's the dogged determination that nothing the enemy does will make you quit or turn back from advancing the Kingdom and from walking in victory! It is not arrogance, but rather true boldness! In Hebrew this is connected with the word for *trust* or *bitcha*, which we mentioned in earlier chapters. This is the kind of boldness that has kept the Israeli Army undefeatable in the face of impossible situations, including when they are grossly outnumbered by enemy troops!

Davka – Do Not Surrender to the Curse!

Mental sickness due to fear and shame is the first result of breaking Elohim's Commandments. We see this in the Garden of Eden when, due to disobedience, the first ADAM (male and female) were filled with fear, shame and unbelief. If you have repented and turned to Yeshua, you must now resist the curse in your life! Mental sickness does not belong to a believer and disciple of Messiah – neither does any other sickness or poverty. Mental sickness of any kind has to be rejected and resisted. This is possible only if you submit to Elohim fully (through Messiah Yeshua) and you surrender your life into His able hands and the ways of His Kingdom.

> *I have been crucified with Messiah; it is no longer I who live, but Messiah lives in me; and the life which I now live in the flesh I live by faith in the Son of God, who loved me and gave Himself for me.*

Galatians 2:20

If you have made this decision, it is now necessary to exercise the *Davka* anointing. If you feel depressed, submit to Yah and to His word and do what it says!

Be indignant with the enemy – make sure he knows that you are not putting up with him anymore; you are no longer putting up with any illness or mental sickness.

And from the days of John the Baptist until now the kingdom of heaven suffers violence, and the violent take it by force.

Matthew 11:12

You must take the Kingdom and His Promises "by force"; in other words, your thoughts must line up with the Promise of Yah (God) and not with your feelings, traumas or circumstances. You have to forcefully reject the curse and walk in the blessing by faith, not feelings.

Holy indignation against the devil is *healthy*! It says, "this far and no more!"

Rejoice on Purpose!

Rejoice always!

1 Thessalonians 5:16

Do you feel *angry* about your circumstances and you do not understand? Defeat the devil with *thanksgiving*!

Now when they began to sing and to praise, the Lord set ambushes against the people of Ammon, Moab, and Mount Seir, who had come against Judah; and they were defeated.

2 Chronicles 20:22

In everything give thanks: for this is the will of God in Messiah Yeshua to you-ward.

1 Thessalonians 5:17

Some people did you wrong and you are bitter? Forgive them *davka*! Then do good to someone. This is how we overcome evil with good.

If your enemy is hungry, give him bread to eat; and if he is thirsty, give him water to drink; for so you will heap coals of fire on his head, and YHVH will reward you.

Proverbs 25:21-22

Are you anxious and stressed? Anxiety brings about depression!

Anxiety in the heart of man causes depression, but a good word makes it glad.

Proverbs 12:25 NKJV

Davka get peaceful! Bind the spirit of anxiety, stress and depression – breathe in and breathe out, begin to pray in tongues and to exalt YHVH. Rejoice in who He is and use all His names (Appendix B). You will see anxiety defeated.

Do you have financial troubles?

Davka seek Yah regarding where to give an offering to break the back of the enemy! The more the enemy tries to rob you, the more you *give on purpose* (Davka) and surely the Ruach will show you how and to whom to give. Generosity is one of the most powerful weapons of warfare.

But a generous man devises generous things, and by generosity he shall stand.

Isaiah 32:8

We are not talking here about indiscriminate giving, as can be seen in people who have a "manic faze" in a bi-polar syndrome, but rather, giving as written in the Holy Scriptures and directed by the Holy Spirit. If we seek to bless others financially, YHVH will direct us and show us. Especially given to those who teach you the Word, as this act of faith, love and honor releases wellbeing into your life.

Let him who is taught the word share in all good things with him who teaches. Do not be deceived, God is not mocked; for whatever a man sows, that he will also reap. For he who sows to his flesh will of the flesh reap corruption, but he who sows to the Spirit will of the Spirit reap everlasting life.

Galatians 6:6-8

"Give and it will be given to you: good measure, pressed down, shaken together, and running over will be put into your bosom. For with the same measure that you use, it will be measured back to you."

Luke 6:38

Are you feeling really bad?

Instead of recoiling into your own pain and suffering, Davka seek to bless someone – help them and minister to them. Self-centeredness leads you into mental sickness and depression, but blessing others makes you whole. Seek to walk in love by losing your life for the sake of others. Seek Yah and He will lead you to find someone you can bless!

And let us not grow weary while doing good, for in due season we shall reap if we do not lose heart. Therefore, as we have opportunity, let us do good to all, especially to those who are of the household of faith.

Galatians 6:9, 10

Satan gets really frustrated when a person *Davka* walks in *victory* when he should be defeated! Beware: he is always tempting you to lose your *faith* and abandon *love*! If he manages to convince you, by his lies, to stop believing Yah, you may then stop walking in Love – this will cause you to lose your mind.

For God has not given us a spirit of fear, but of power and of love and of a sound mind.

2 Timothy 1:7

Walking In Love Davka Makes You Whole

Judge not, that you be not judged. For with what judgment you judge, you will be judged; and with the measure you use, it will be measured back to you.

Matthew 7:1

Unforgiveness and bitter judgment bring torment and defilement!

*Looking carefully lest anyone fall short of the grace of God;
lest any root of bitterness springing up cause trouble, and by
this many become defiled.*

Hebrews 12:15

The most tormented and sick people, both physically and mentally, are those who judge others and are bitter against others who have disappointed or hurt them. I cannot emphasize this enough: unforgiveness and bitter judgment is a thief and a murderer!

This is why Yeshua warns us that if we don't forgive others we shall not be forgiven by Elohim (Matthew 6:15). It is the key for our wellbeing. We can try to keep all the laws of Elohim, but if we fail to walk in forgiveness, compassion and love, we will be sick in body, mind and spirit. We will be under the curse rather than under His Blessing. Offering forgiveness does not mean that we agree with the evil done – it only means that we are willing to humble our hearts, realizing that we are not any better than anyone else. Therefore we forgive, just like we need forgiveness countless times! Forgiveness is a command not any less than "thou shall not murder" or "keep the Shabbat Holy."

*For if you forgive men their trespasses, your heavenly Father
will also forgive you, but if you do not forgive men their
trespasses, neither will your Father forgive your trespasses.*

Matthew 6:14-15

Love cannot be defeated – if you pursue love, Love will pursue you! Walk the extra mile and you will always be well. Walk *on purpose* in love!

You have heard that it was said, 'You shall love your neighbor and hate your enemy,' but I say to you, love your enemies, bless those who curse you, do good to those who hate you, and pray for those who spitefully use you and persecute you, that you may be sons of your Father in heaven; for He makes His sun rise on the evil and on the good, and sends rain on the just and on the unjust. For if you love those who love you, what reward have you? Do not even the tax collectors do the same? And if you greet your brethren only, what do you do more than others? Do not even the tax collectors do so? Therefore you shall be perfect, just as your Father in heaven is perfect.

Matthew 5:43-48

Almost every mental problem can be connected to some bitterness or "love failure." Embracing love, just like Yeshua embraced the Cross, will cause us to walk in total victory at all times. Do not ever expect people to reward you, for if they fail to do so, you will grow bitter and disappointed. Love because Elohim is Love, and He will reward you.

Most people expect others to love them and then grow bitter when they don't meet their "love expectations." Stay busy loving others (relying on help from His Holy Spirit); as you sow, you will also reap, but remember that true love is selfless – in other words, the motivation is *pure.* You walk in Love simply because it pleases YHVH and because you are imitating Yeshua's selfless sacrificial life and death. False expectations from others will always lead to bitterness.

Therefore, whatever you want men to do to you, do also to them, for this is the Law and the Prophets.

Matthew 7:12

Love never fails.

1 Corinthians 13:8a

Satan is a liar!

You are of your father the devil, and the desires of your father you want to do. He was a murderer from the beginning, and does not stand in the truth, because there is no truth in him. When he speaks a lie, he speaks from his own resources, for he is a liar and the father of it.

John 8:44

Satan is a liar! Do not believe any negative symptoms or circumstances! You may acknowledge them and evaluate if there are *real* causes for the way you feel physically or mentally, but the ultimate cure for all of them is the *truth* of Yah's Word. You will overcome lies using His Word, coupled with the guidance of the Holy Spirit on some practical things to do. You may need to change your diet, take vitamins, forgive someone, sleep and rest, do exercise, even receive healing or deliverance from demons. Remember to declare the Word over your situation (in every case!) and especially to walk in love at all times.

We are not discarding the importance of practical help, but when you realize that Satan is a cunning liar, you will not get discouraged and lose your faith – causing you to eventually speak, repeating his toxic words of defeat rather than Yah's uplifting Words of Promise!

Acknowledge your pain and any symptoms, but do not trust them – and certainly do not let them rule your life! Symptoms and pain will come and go but knowing the Word of Truth will make you free from pain and anguish!

And you shall know the truth, and the truth shall make you free.

John 8:32

Surely He (Yeshua) has borne our griefs and carried our sorrows; yet we esteemed Him stricken, smitten by God, and afflicted, but He was wounded for our transgressions, He was bruised for our iniquities; the chastisement for our peace (shalom-wellbeing) was upon Him, and by His stripes we are healed.

Isaiah 53:4-5

King David acknowledged his difficult circumstances but chose to encourage himself in YHVH and commanded his soul to praise Him *Davka*! On purpose!

Bless YHVH, O my soul; and all that is within me, bless His holy name! Bless YHVH, O my soul, and forget not all His benefits.

Psalm 103:1-2

Declare out loud: "Yeshua, you carried all my griefs and sorrows, so I refuse to carry them! I give them all to you and I bless YHVH by faith all the days of my life! HalleluYah!

Speak Faith

I shall not die, but live, and declare the works of YHVH.

Psalm 118:17

Davka! On purpose speak *faith* in every situation, even if you feel like dying! Declare, "I will not die, but live and declare the works of Adonai!" Declare it with your mouth the whole day, with gusto: sing it, dance it, and shout it, "I will not die, but live and declare the works of Adonai!"

CHAPTER ELEVEN

Faith Is Work!

The only way to be whole mentally is to exchange our fleshly mind for the *mind of Messiah*!

"For who has known the mind of the Lord, that he will instruct Him? But we have the mind of Messiah."

1 Corinthians 2:16

Therefore they said to Him, "What shall we do, so that we may work the works of Elohim-God?" Yeshua answered and said to them, "This is the work of Elohim, that you believe in Him whom He has sent."

John 6:28-29

Faith is a work that begins in our thoughts, then appears in our speech, actions and attitudes. We must work it through – it is not automatic! It is actually a Fruit of the Spirit (Galatians 5:22,23) and like all fruit it develops out of well fertilized soil. That manure or fertilizer is normally 'stinking situations' that can make us or break us. If we respond in faith, the fruit of faith will develop – and with it comes a healthy mind.

It's Easier to Take a Pill, But Is it the Life You Want?

When pills don't work, then what do you do? There are countless people taking psychiatric medication, but they do not really feel good at all. Many of them kill themselves while on medications. Others gain weight in a dangerous way or harm their immune system because of the side effects of these potent drugs.

Some people have been greatly helped by prescribed psychiatric drugs, but it always comes with a price tag, and that price tag is very high.

For the unbelievers, psychiatric drugs are a life saver in some cases, and a life destroyer in others, but for believers who have the inheritance of Yeshua's Blood and YHVH's Word, we have clearly outlined that there is another option which can be exercised even if you are already taking medications. Eventually your doctor may see the change and be courageous enough to lower the dosage or remove them altogether, but do not worry about that – just do the Work of Faith and the results will follow!

Do the Work of Faith & Inherit a Life of Wholeness!

Stop following your feelings: believe His Word and follow the Holy Spirit as He leads!

I have the option to choose how I feel each day. Even though I may be feeling low or discouraged or fearful or anguished, as I unburden my feelings on YHVH (my Heavenly Psychologist), I then choose to trust Him and His Word. As I pray in tongues and especially sing in tongues, I am elevated from my own feelings to *his mind* – and then healing flows into my mind!

Walking low or walking high, walking sick or walking whole, walking anxious or in shalom, it all depends on YOU. It has been given to us to walk in the *blessing* or in the *curse*: we choose!, but if we choose *the blessing*, we must be determined to walk in it *Davka* (On Purpose), and by faith before we will see the manifestation.

An Important Disclaimer

We have to be totally submitted to Yah, to His Word, to His Ruach (Spirit), and to those who YHVH has placed around us to help us, be it spouses, parents, pastors or leaders!

Walking in faith is not walking in presumption or arrogance, and the *fruit* is obvious as the fruit is *love*. Love brings about emotional stability and does not harm others.

But the fruit of the Spirit is love, joy, peace, patience, kindness, goodness, faithfulness, gentleness, self-control; against such things there is no law. Now those who belong to Messiah Yeshua have crucified the flesh with its passions and desires.

Galatians 5:22-24

The Faith of Abraham Leaves the Familiar Behind!

Leaving behind mental sickness (along with all its physical symptoms of insomnia, dry mouth, etc.) is much like Abram leaving his idolatrous family behind in Haran. Elohim told him to follow Him and to go to a Land of Promise that Abram did not know. He did not give him a map, but told him to just start walking by faith, promising Abram great blessings and great protection!

> *Now YHVH said to Abram, "Go forth from your country, and from your relatives. And from your father's house, to the land which I will show you; and I will make you a great nation, and I will bless you, and make your name great; and so you shall be a blessing; and I will bless those who bless you, and the one who curses you I will curse. And in you all the families of the earth will be blessed."*

> Genesis 12:1-3

Leaving the familiarity of a sick mind, sickology, psychology, humanism, self-centeredness, and the religion of unbelief requires *faith*, and only a faith like Abram will do. He had to leave all that was familiar behind him to venture into the unknown!

How did he do it? *By* faith, Davka, on purpose!

Have you been a fearful unbeliever until now? Davka, on purpose, decide to walk as a bold, courageous believer and disciple of Messiah! Have you been self-centered until now because of your pain and suffering? Davka, on purpose, decide to be a blessing to others and forget about yourself for a while. You have probably given yourself most of your attention already, now give it to YHVH, and serve Him by blessing others in spite of your personal suffering.

Nothing will keep you more sane than being busy at being a blessing and walking selflessly. Whatever you feed grows, whatever you starve dies. Stop feeding your pain and negative emotions! Instead, feed your spirit with the Word and Prayer. Feed your *mouth* with His Word, not your own words of defeat, then watch His Angels minister on your behalf!

Bless YHVH, you His angels, Mighty in strength, who perform His word, obeying the voice of His word!

Psalm 103:20

If you speak words of unbelief and you declare sickness, bad feelings, or symptoms, demons will come and make sure that these feelings and symptoms stay. We will eat the fruit of our words whether life or death!

Death and life are in the power of the tongue, and those who love it will eat its fruit.

Proverbs 18:21

Removing the Mystery of Schizophrenia

Nearly every time psychiatrists do not know how to categorize a mental sickness they call it *Schizoaffective Disorder.* They will often prescribe strong anti-psychotic drugs that have many side effects, adding to the anti-depressants, mood stabilizers and sleeping pills already being taken. Often more pills are needed to help counteract the symptoms of all the other medication; But what is Schizoaffective Disorder or Schizophrenia? It was a real challenge to find the meaning of this word, which is so widely used by psychiatrists. It was coined only 100 years ago, and this is the meaning:

1912, from Modern Latin, literally "a splitting of the mind," from German Schizophrenie, coined in 1910 by Swiss psychiatrist Eugen Bleuler (1857-1939), from Greek skhizein "to split" (see schizo-) + phren (genitive phrenos) "diaphragm, heart, mind," of unknown origin. (etymonline.com/index.php?term=schizophrenia, Accessed 22 Sept, 2016)

Schizo: splitting or dividing; Phrenia: diaphragm, heart or mind. It literally means a divided mind! A divided heart or a divided diaphragm (that is where you feel anxiety and that is where your spirit is – in your belly or innermost being)

He who believes in Me, as the Scripture said, 'From his innermost being will flow rivers of living water.'

John 7:38

Long ago YHVH spoke through the first Pastor of Jerusalem, Yaakov (James), the natural brother of Yeshua, saying:

But if any of you lacks wisdom, let him ask of God, who gives to all generously and without reproach, and it will be given to him, but he must ask in faith without any doubting, for the one who doubts is like the surf of the sea, driven and tossed by the wind. For that man ought not to expect that he will receive anything from the Lord, being a double-minded man, unstable in all his ways.

Yaakov (James) 1:5-8

A person who doubts Yah's wisdom and leans into his/her own understanding, will be double minded (schizophrenic) and unstable (bi-polar) in all his ways. Doubt and unbelief are the root cause of Schizophrenia!

All people are under the curse of the Tree of Knowledge of Good and Evil. That tree immediately brings about a split personality and schizophrenia. We are born under that curse. For some it is more acute than others because of family curses, especially those who are born into families who embrace witchcraft, idolatry, Free Masonry, and various kinds of secret societies which are all Luciferian religions. If you were born into a family with that background, the curse will manifest up to the 4th generation – it is necessary to do generational repentance for the sins of idolatry of your ancestors (including those from Catholicism, Buddhism and Hinduism).

For I, YHVH your God, am a jealous God, visiting the iniquity of the fathers on the children, and on the third and the fourth generations of those who hate Me.

Deuteronomy 5:9b

After recognizing and asking forgiveness for the sins of your ancestors and for your own sins, accept and embrace Yah's forgiveness and break the power of Schizophrenia over your life. Bind the familiar curse spirits of Schizophrenia, doubt and unbelief, and cast them out of your life and immediate family! exercise authority if you have given your whole life to Yeshua. Praise YHVH and declare His Word of Promise about having a sound mind.

For God has not given us a spirit of fear, but of power and of love and of a sound mind.

2 Timothy 1:7

Walk Davka, on purpose, in faith in spite of all symptoms and circumstances. Do not open the door to unbelief. Whenever you do not understand, just pray for understanding and meditate on His Word. *Rest* in Him as you pray in tongues and worship Him. Trust Him like a baby trusts the mother who nurses it. (Psalm 131)

Unbelievers and doubters can never experience freedom from Schizophrenia, but those who *perservere* in applying what I have written in this book will walk in wholeness, by faith and not by feelings, by faith and not by sight!

Some symptoms may not disappear right away, but if you persevere to walk by faith in His Word, declaring what He says above your symptoms, you will experience a breakthrough! Be more stubborn than the devil!

Therefore submit to God. Resist the devil and he will flee from you.

Yaakov (James) 4:7

Stay humble and in faith. You can only resist the devil once you have submitted to Elohim through His Word and Spirit, and to those spiritual leaders who watch over your soul. Sometimes these spiritual leaders are parents or spouses.

Pride and unbelief will keep you schizophrenic while humility and faith will heal you!

Many people who are prone to bi-polar and/or schizophrenia have the tendency to be presumptuous, rebellious and arrogant. While everyone must be on guard in these areas in our lives, those who have been plagued with the above mentioned sicknesses will have to be doubly watchful against pride and arrogance. Spiritual pride must be even more diligently guarded against. True faith submits to Divinely appointed leaders, spouses and parents. *Listen to godly instruction* and do not be wise in your own eyes!

Perseverance Is the Key

Once you are determined to be *free* and *whole*, do not give in or give up! In fact, do not even give it a thought! Just continue walking by faith, obeying the Father, being a blessing to others, resting and unburdening in Him as you pray, declaring the Word of Promise, smiling and rejoicing on purpose – it *always* works! Ha, ha, ha! Satan and Schizophrenia are unmasked and de-demystified forever!

Faith Speaks, Acts, & Shows on Purpose: Davka!

Doubt your doubts and trust YHVH!

Trust in YHVH with all your heart and do not lean on your own understanding. In all your ways acknowledge Him, and He will make your paths straight.

Proverbs 3:5-6

A Declaration of Commitment

You will also declare a thing, and it will be established for you; so light will shine on your ways.

Job 22:28

Now pray the following out loud. Be bold and stand like a warrior somewhere in an open place and *shout* this:

"I have decided to leave Schizophrenia and all mental sickness behind! I have decided to follow Yeshua, His Word and His Holy Spirit – not my mind, my feelings, my emotions or any of my family curses! I choose to believe on purpose, Davka! I choose to rejoice always on purpose, Davka! I choose to thank Yah always on purpose, Davka! I choose to forgive everyone on purpose, Davka! I choose to walk in love and under the Blessing on purpose, Davka! No matter what – against all odds, regardless of symptoms, pains or circumstances – I have decided to put my trust in YHVH, His Word, His Nature and His ability and not in my own understanding, mind, opinion, past experiences, traumas, mistakes or interpretations!

I choose to believe what He says above all other evil reports even though they may sound 'professional.' And I choose to declare YHVH's report and Word above any other reports about my condition! In fact I choose to walk as an HEIR of Mental Health because I have chosen to wear the Mind of Messiah at all times!

I choose to command my thoughts to be CAPTIVE to Messiah daily and reaffirm this as many times a day as it is needed!

I choose to confront all my fears and anxieties and to expose them to the Light of the Word of Yah. I choose to walk in love, the Perfect Love of Yah that casts out all fear. There is no fear in love. I do not entertain a spirit of fear or anxiety, but I totally embrace love, power and a sound mind!

I have chosen to believe all things promised to me by Yah and His Word, even if the manifestation takes longer than I desire. I trust Him for the timing, and I trust Him for the way it will manifest! I choose to receive by faith, regardless of the symptoms in my life, and I will obey him concerning any practical and natural steps to take regarding my condition on top of the spiritual ones.

I have declared an all-out war against mental sickness and I have won because ALL mental sickness was nailed to the Cross of Messiah 2000 years ago and I have inherited the Mind of Messiah for all eternity!"

Do You Believe?

If you now believe that having a sound, healthy mind is your inheritance through Yeshua's sacrifice, take it, wear it and never, never look back!

Declare with me:

I take the Mind of Messiah and I give Him my old sick mind – I declare this in Yeshua's name! Amen!

But He was wounded for our transgressions, He was bruised for our iniquities; the chastisement for our wellbeing was upon Him, and by His stripes we are healed.

Isaiah 55:5

CHAPTER TWELVE

Caregivers: Buckle Yourself First

*The second is this: 'Love your neighbor as yourself.' There
is no commandment greater than these."*

Mark 12:31

This chapter is dedicated mostly to those who are taking
care of people who have been labeled as mentally sick
or psychiatric cases diagnosed with Depression, Bi-
Polar, Schizophrenia, ADHD and the like. Most of the time
the ones who get all the attention are those who are "suffering
from mental problems", but the truth is, the ones who suffer the
most are the immediate family and the care givers. Mistakenly,
very little (if any) attention is given to those who are constantly
battling for their loved ones. It is high time to change this state
of affairs by placing greater emphasis toward giving support
and guidance to those who have been the support system of the
mentally ill. They need to be undergirded by our love, using His

Word daily to combat discouragement and weariness.

In past chapters I have related to those who are battling with mental problems, giving much instruction that, if applied, can bring anyone to a place of wholeness. Nothing is stronger or more effective than Elohim's Word. We must remember that He created the Heavens and the Earth with His Word; therefore, if anyone submits to His Word and applies His Word to every circumstance of life, there will be a breakthrough. Yeshua even cast out demons by the Word!

> *When evening came, they brought to Him many who were demon-possessed; and He cast out the spirits with a word, and healed all who were ill.*

> Matthew 8:16

Stubbornness & Rebellion

For rebellion is as the sin of witchcraft, and stubbornness is as iniquity and idolatry. Because you have rejected the word of the Lord, He also has rejected you from being king."

> 1 Samuel 15:23 NKJV

Though the solution to mental problems is clear and quite simple, yet the application of it seems to be a big challenge, because it depends on the self-will of the sick individual. The biggest problem of most mentally sick people is that they are terribly stubborn and rebellious. They will argue endlessly instead of simply submitting to the Word and to authority. It takes a lot of breaking and Divine Revelation for a mentally sick person to surrender to YHVH, to His Word and to Spiritual Authorities around them. This can be a long arduous process, not because the cure is not available, but rather because of the stubborn self-will of the individual. Elohim gave a free-self-will to Adam in the Garden of Eden, and ever since, He has allowed people to make their own choices. Our prayers avail much so that Abba can work with the very stubborn self-will of our loved ones, but we cannot change them, as much as we would love to! They have to CHOOSE to submit to Him and to His treatment. Even the demon possessed man from the Gadarenes had to make his choice prior to his deliverance of a Legion (10,000) of demons – he threw himself at the feet of Yeshua! Once a mentally sick person throws himself at the feet of Yeshua and submits to those who have Yeshua's Word and Power, they will be set free!!

Then they came to the other side of the sea, to the country of the Gadarenes and when He had come out of the boat, immediately there met Him out of the tombs a man with an unclean spirit, who had his dwelling among the tombs; and no one could bind him not even with chains, because he had often been bound with shackles and chains. And the chains had been pulled apart by him, and the shackles broken in pieces; neither could anyone tame him. And always, night and day, he was in the mountains and in the tombs, crying out and cutting himself with stones.

Mark 5:1-5

Today this man would have been labeled bi-polar or schizophrenic and he would have been locked in a closed ward of a Psychiatric Hospital and filled with medication. Even though he was completely crazy – mentally imbalanced, demon possessed by ten thousand demons, obviously dangerous to himself and to others – notice one thing: he still had a *free*-self-will. He was still free to choose to worship Yeshua and be set free!

When he saw Yeshua from afar, he ran and worshiped Him.

Mark 5:6

He opposed a legion of ten thousand demons and worshipped the Master! Even though everything in him was opposing this act, he *chose* to surrender. Until our loved ones *choose* to surrender in spite of their condition, we are faced with a reality that is *very* challenging. Yeshua would have not set that man free had he not worshipped him. He only delivered those who came to Him or those who were so helpless that they were brought by others –, but none were stubbornly resistant to Him!

And the whole multitude sought to touch Him, for power went out from Him and healed them all.

Luke 6:19

Many times as I go to the nations, I am privileged to be used to set depressed and other mentally sick people free. They come to the meetings seeking help from the Master and they receive it. Yet, I have to deal with some of my own loved ones who stubbornly resist Yeshua, His Love and Word and they cannot be healed. It can be extremely frustrating, but we need to realize that we cannot force people into salvation and wholeness. That is a work that belongs to YHVH alone, and our prayers of faith definitely help, even if it takes a long time.

Buckle Yourself First

The second is this: 'Love your neighbor as yourself.' There is no commandment greater than these."

Mark 12:31

The family members who are in a life and death, wearing and tearing, battle with their loved ones can also come to a point of dangerous exhaustion. This is exactly what the devil wants. He wants to destroy as much as possible, and so he uses rebellious and stubborn people to lash out at their families. As much as we love those who are still resisting the Holy Spirit and Yeshua's Cure, we must also love ourselves. Whenever we fly in an airplane, they always tell us to buckle ourselves first. They instruct us, in case of an emergency, to adjust our oxygen mask *first* before we care for those minors or dependents who are flying with us. This is exactly what we need to do concerning our relationship with, and caregiving of, those loved ones who demand superhuman attention and strength: We must "buckle" ourselves *first*!

Love your neighbor as *yourself*!

If you do not take proper care of yourself, you will collapse, and then it will be worse for you and for the loved one you are caring for. Most people are afraid of caring for themselves

– taking days off, pampering themselves, going on holidays by *themselves*, etc. – because they feel that this would make them "selfish." In fact, those loved ones for whom you are caring, because of their lack of mental health, will make a point of telling you that you are selfish, and will accuse you of the most terrible things. Remember, Satan works through accusations and condemnation – so, if after pouring out your life to assist someone who is mentally sick you are still accused, this must be dealt with in a wise manner.

> *Then I heard a loud voice saying in heaven, "Now salvation, and strength, and the kingdom of our God, and the power of His Messiah have come, for the accuser of our brethren, who accused them before our God day and night, has been cast down.*

Revelation 12:10

- Recognize the source of the accusation
- Discern emotional manipulation and co-dependence
- Be honest with yourself and with YHVH about your emotions, but choose   faith
- Shake off the viper (of condemnation) like Paul did in the Isle of Malta
- Take a day off and have some holy *fun*!
- Rotate care givers so you can get some distance from your "patient"
- Bask in the presence of the Holy Spirit with your favorite worship music
- Pray in tongues and declare the Word of Promise for *you*!

- Have others pray and minister to *you*. Enjoy life in spite of their condition!
- Obey Yah's Call for your life even if it means that others will take your place as caregiver (even a mental hospital if there is no other choice)

Periodical Maintenance

Thus the heavens and the earth, and all the host of them, were finished. And on the seventh day God ended His work which He had done, and He rested on the seventh day from all His work which He had done.

Genesis 2:1

I cannot stress enough the importance of periodical maintenance for yourself! Why is it that we take care of our cars better than ourselves? When cars ran out of gasoline, they can't go on, period! They have to refuel. When you run out of joy, patience and shalom, you can't go on either.

You have to refuel by going into Yah's Presence, to a Worship Meeting, to a Faith Conference, to the beach, to a good movie, for a long walk or something else that restores your soul. When the battery of a car runs out, you have to buy a new one. In the same way, when your 'love batteries' run out, you have to get a new one from the Presence of the Holy Spirit. In Israel every 10,000 kms we have to bring the car to the shop in order to change the oil – in the same way, every once in a while you have to go on holidays and forget all about your 'patient.' If you don't take these instructions seriously, sooner or later you will collapse!

Beware of Kryptonite – Rotate Caregivers!

You are not the only one in the world who can help. Pray and YHVH will show you other people. You can get help from family, friends, or your church. If there is no other option, you can hire someone or use the services of a mental hospital. When your loved one says, "I only want *you*", it is time to *run* from this manipulation tactic. Unless you break that ungodly soul tie, it will bring you down!! You are not God! The sooner that you realize this the better. When you see that your loved one plays with your emotions and you can't resist it, they have become to you like "kryptonite to Superman." Once that happens, you are too emotionally weak to maintain correct boundaries, and you can burn out. In this case, you have to detach yourself and have the System or other people take over. Recognize when such a relationship has become utterly unhealthy and acknowledge it can destroy you. Whenever someone has such influence on you that you can't say, "No", thereby, keeping your God given individuality and personal boundaries, you need to detach until you are restored.

> *"Come to Me, all you who labor and are heavy laden, and*
> *I will give you rest. Take My yoke upon you and learn from*
> *Me, for I am gentle and lowly in heart, and you will find*

rest for your souls. For My yoke is easy and My burden is light."

Matthew 11:28-30

YHVH will work with you in *your* reality and He will give you *rest* as you apply the instructions that are written here. You can have abundance of life and great joy even if your loved one is still stubbornly resisting Him and His mental cure! The psychiatric system, in this case, is of great help. Faith instructions bring the cure but can only help those who willingly surrender to Yeshua. All the other ones need to get help from the medical system, and this is substantial grace. Do not feel guilty. Do not feel as if you have failed to help them or as if Yah's Word and Power have failed! Yeshua could do no miracles in Nazareth because of the familiarity and the unbelief! Your loved ones have their self-will, and their road to walk until Yah's Promises come to pass. You can't walk their road for them.

Remember that in order to love your neighbor in action, you have to love and care for yourself!

The Priestly Blessing

YHVH bless you and keep you,

YHVH make His face to shine upon you,

And be gracious unto you,

YHVH lift up His countenance to you,

And give you shalom.

Numbers 6:22-26

Contact Us

For more books on this and other subjects by Archbishop Dr. Dominiquae Bierman, visit our website: www.kad-esh.org.

Email us at info@kad-esh.org, or call us in the USA at 1-972-301-7087or in Israel +972-52-3422673

Invite Dr. Dominiquae Bierman to speak to your congregation or group. You can also organize a conference in your area that will change the lives of many. Call us at the above numbers or write us an email to schedule meetings.

APPENDIX A

What Is Replacement Theology?

Replacement theology called for a complete separation from all the Jewish Roots of Christianity. It replaced the original Biblical Sabbath, Biblical Feasts, Name and the identity of the Messiah as a Jew. This theology was established as Church doctrine through the Council of Nicea in 325 AD by the Bizantine-Roman Emperor, Constantine, and the ensuing gentile Church Fathers. Replacement Theology is the culprit behind most of the persecutions, pogroms and mass genocide of Jews between the 4th Century and the Shoa (Holocaust) by Nazi Germany during WW2.

For a complete understanding of this important topic, download Dr. Dominiquae's free book, The MAP Revolution by visiting www.kad-esh.org/shop.

APPENDIX B

The Names of God

- Yah – God's private name
- YHVH (pronounced *Yahveh*)– The I Am
- Adonai – Lord
- Elohim – God the Creator
- Yeshua – The Savior and Redeemer Messiah
- ABBA – Our Father
- Yahveh Rofeh – God my Doctor
- Yahveh Roi – God my Shepherd
- Yahveh Shama – God who is there for me
- Yahveh Shalom – The God of peace and wellbeing
- Yahveh Tsidkeinu – God my Righteousness
- Yahveh Mekadesh – God who sanctifies me
- Nasich Shalom – Yeshua, Prince of my shalom
- Ruach Hakodesh – Holy Spirit

Appendix C

Other Books

Order now online: www.kad-esh.org/shop/

The MAP Revolution (Free E-Book)
Find Out Why Revival Does Not Come... Yet!

The Identity Theft
The Return of the 1st Century Messiah

The Key of Abraham
The Blessing, or the Curse!

ATG: Addicts Turning to God
The Biblical Way to Handle Addicts and Addictions

The Healing Power of the Roots
It's a Matter of Life or Death!

Grafted In
It's Time to Take the Nation's!

Sheep Nations
It's Time to Take the Nations!

Restoring the Glory: The Original Way
The Ancient Paths Rediscovered

Stormy Weather
Judgment Has Already Begun, Revival is Knocking at the Door

Yeshua is the Name
The Important Restoration of the Original
Hebrew Name of the Messiah

Defeating Depression
This Book is a Kiss from Heaven!

Let's Get Healthy, Saints!
The Biblical Guide to Nutrition

Yes!
The Dramatic Salvation of
Archbishop Dr. Dominiquae Bierman

Eradicating the Cancer of Religion
Hint: All People Have It

Restoration of Holy Giving
Releasing the True 1,000 Fold Blessing

Vision Negev
The Awesome Restoration of the Sephardic Jews

The Woman Factor by Rabbi Baruch Bierman
Freedom From Womanphobia

The Revival of the Third Day (Free E-Book)
The Return to Yeshua the Jewish Messiah

Music Albums
www.kad-esh.org/shop/

The Key of Abraham

Abba Shebashamayim

Uru

Retorno

Get Equipped & Partner with Us

Global Revival MAP (GRM) Israeli Bible School
Take the most comprehensive video Bible school online that
focuses on dismantling replacement theology.
For more information or to order, please contact us:

www.grmbibleschool.com

grm@dominiquaebierman.com

United Nations for Israel Movement

We invite you to join us as a member and partner with $25 a
month, which supports the advancing of this End time vision
that will bring true unity to the body of the Messiah. We will

see the One New Man form, witness the restoration of Israel, and take part in the birthing of SHEEP NATIONS. Today is an exciting time to be serving Him!

www.unitednationsforisrael.org

info@unitednationsforisrael.org

Global Re-Education Initiative (GRI)
Against Anti-Semitism

Discover the Jewishness of Jesus and defeat Christian anti-Semitism with this online video course to see revival in your nation!

www.against-antisemitism.com

info@against-antisemitism.com

Join Our Annual Israel Tours

Travel through the Holy Land and watch the Hebrew Holy Scriptures come alive.

www.kad-esh.org/tours-and-events/

To Send Offerings to Support our Work

Your help keeps this mission of restoration going far and wide.

www.kad-esh.org/donations

CONTACT US

Archbishop Dr. Dominiquae & Rabbi Baruch Bierman

Kad-Esh MAP Ministries | www.kad-esh.org

info@kad-esh.org

United Nations for Israel | www.unitednationsforisrael.org
info@unitednationsforisrael.org

Zion's Gospel Press | shalom@zionsgospel.com
52 Tuscan Way, Ste 202-412, 32092 St. Augustine Florida,
USA | +1-972-301-7087